EXCEPTIONALITY, 8(3), 145–148

PREFACE

Including the Functional Behavioral Assessment Technology in Schools

George Sugai and Robert H. Horner
Center on Positive Behavioral Interventions and Supports[1]
University of Oregon

With the 1997 amendments to the Individuals With Disabilities Education Act (IDEA), many important practices and policies were added to the implementation of special education in our public schools. In particular, behavioral intervention planning and positive behavioral supports now must be based on information obtained through the functional behavioral assessment (FBA) process. Although the FBA requirements are laudatory, IDEA 1997 provides limited descriptions and policy regarding the "best practices" implementation of the FBA process. Efforts have been made to translate policy and move research to practice (see OSEP Center on Positive Behavioral Interventions and Supports, 1999); however, implementation specificity regarding the FBA process has not been developed well.

PURPOSE AND OVERVIEW

The purpose of this special issue of *Exceptionality* is to provide educators with information that increases the efficiency, effectiveness, and relevance of the FBA process and prevents the development of misrules about the implementation of the FBA process. In

Requests for reprints should be sent to George Sugai, 5262 University of Oregon, Eugene, OR 97403–5262. E-mail: sugai@oregon.uoregon.edu

[1]The Center on Positive Behavioral Interventions and Supports is supported by a grant from the Office of Special Education Programs, with additional funding from the Safe and Drug Free Schools Program, U.S. Department of Education (Grant No. H326S980003). Opinions expressed herein are ours and do not necessarily reflect the position of the U.S. Department of Education, and such endorsements should not be inferred.

the first article, George Sugai, Teri Lewis-Palmer, and Shanna Hagan-Burke provide an overview of the definition, critical elements, and steps of the FBA process. This overview emphasizes a "best" or "preferred" practices approach based on an empirical and theoretical foundation that begins with Skinner's (1938) seminal work.

In their article, Deanne Crone and Rob Horner describe the conceptual and empirical foundations that have shaped and influenced the development of current FBA process. In addition to tracing the historical roots of FBA, they also emphasize the importance of understanding the contexts of today's schools and changing the way we think about assessment of and intervention with problem behavior.

Brennan Wilcox and Rud and Ann Turnbull ask us to look at the policy implications and practices of the FBA process. They point to the important interplay between policy and practice within the context of special and general education settings.

Joshua Harrower, Lise Fox, Glen Dunlap, and Don Kincaid focus our attention on the FBA process from an early intervention perspective. They provide us with considerations and guidelines for utilizing the FBA process with young children with challenging behavior and as an important component of a comprehensive preventative approach.

Rob Horner, George Sugai, Anne Todd, and Teri Lewis-Palmer give us a technical brief on the key elements of behavior intervention plan development. They emphasize the importance of using teams of competent educators to develop behavior support plans that define how the environment will change to help the student reduce problem behavior, improve prosocial behavior, and become more successful at school.

In the final article, Wayne Sailor, Rachel Freeman, Jody Britten, Amy McCart, Christopher Smith, Terry Scott, and Mike Nelson discuss the importance of improving how educators are taught about the FBA process to high levels of fluency. They provide guidelines for both preservice and in-service instruction on FBA.

PREVENTING MISRULES

A common message across all of the articles in this special issue is the effective, efficient, and relevant use of the FBA process to prevent the development of misrules about FBA. Misrules result when insufficient, inaccurate, or unsupported information is used to guide decision making and implementation. The articles in this special issue emphasize the prevention of the following five FBA misrules.

"All FBA Information Must Be Collected in the Same Way Every Time"

Although the FBA process is basically the same across situations, FBA information can be collected in multiple ways (i.e., archival review, checklists, interviews, direct observation) from multiple sources (e.g., students, teachers, parents) and in multiple contexts (e.g., classrooms, homes, playgrounds). The selection of data collection methods, sources, and contexts should be based on collaborative decision-making and problem-solving processes in which consideration is given to what is already known, what needs to be determined, and how much evidence is needed to confirm decisions—all within the context of the individual needs of the student and his or her learning and living environments.

"Everyone Has to Know How to Conduct an FBA"

Although everyone (e.g., teachers, parents, administrators, paraprofessionals, counselors) should know what the purpose, outcomes, and general steps of the FBA process are, only a small number of individuals must have high competence, broad experience, and skill fluency to lead a team of individuals through the FBA process and conduct each step. Fluency is acquired through completion of multiple supervised FBAs. These same individuals must establish systems and procedures that support high accuracy of sustained implementation (e.g., data collection and evaluation).

"FBA Is It"

The FBA process leads a team of individuals toward a specific behavior intervention plan that gives careful consideration to the specific conditions that occasion and maintain problem behavior and to the modification of the environment to promote displays of more effective and efficient prosocial behavior. For students with significant challenging problem behaviors, comprehensive and targeted behavior support plans also must include consideration and development of supports that extend beyond specific behavioral intervention plans (e.g., family support, medical or pharmaceutical interventions, mental health supports, juvenile justice involvement). Systems of care and wraparound processes should be used to facilitate the development of comprehensive behavior supports.

"FBAs Are Conducted to Determine Eligibility, Placement, or Manifestation Determination"

Although information from the FBA process can be used by teams of educators and parents to assist in decisions regarding special education eligibility, placement, and determination of whether a behavior is related to an individual's disability, the main purpose of engaging in the FBA process is to improve our understanding of the problem behavior and the contexts in which the behaviors are more and less likely to be observed. Most important, the main outcome of the FBA process is the development of effective, efficient, and relevant behavior intervention plans.

"FBA Is Only Used With Students With Disabilities"

Although the FBA process has become a prominent and necessary aspect of special education in the public schools, the FBA process can be applied whenever an improved understanding of behavior is desired or a behavior intervention plan needs to be developed. The use of the FBA process is not limited to special education; it can be used (a) with any observable behavior; (b) for both problem and desired behavior; (c) with children, adolescents, and adults with and without disabilities; and (d) in home, school, and community settings.

The FBA process is an important tool for educators to improve their understanding of problem behavior and guide the development of useful behavior intervention plans. However, the FBA process does not do everything, and it has specific uses that have empirical and theoretical supports. More important, the ability for a school to implement the FBA process with high accuracy over time requires a solid schooliwide continuum of positive behavioral support that works for all students and staff, and a team of educators who have high fluency with the FBA process.

REFERENCES

Individuals With Disabilities Education Act Amendments of 1997, 20 U.S.C. § 1400 *et seq.* (1997).

OSEP Center on Positive Behavioral Interventions and Supports. (1999). *Applying positive behavioral support and functional assessment in schools* [Technical Assistance Guide 1]. Eugene: University of Oregon.

Skinner, B. F. (1938). *The behavior of organisms: An experimental analysis.* New York: Appleton-Century-Crofts.

EXCEPTIONALITY, *8*(3), 149–160

ARTICLES

Overview of the Functional Behavioral Assessment Process

George Sugai, Teri Lewis-Palmer, and Shanna Hagan-Burke
College of Education
University of Oregon

The research literature is replete with examples that support the use of the functional behavioral assessment (FBA) process. In addition, the 1997 amendments to the Individuals With Disabilities Education Act have recognized the importance of the FBA process for students who display significant problem behavior in schools. However, clarity about the specific definition and features of the FBA process is just beginning to be developed. The purpose of this article is to provide a general description of the features and steps of the FBA process.

Although the 1997 amendments to the Individuals With Disabilities Education Act (IDEA) emphasized the use of functional behavioral assessment (FBA) in schools, the idea of looking at behavior within the context in which it is observed has been in the literature since the early 1900s. Discussions about functional analysis and functional relationships began with the early writings and works of Ivan Pavlov, John Watson, Edward Thorndike, Fred Keller, B. F. Skinner, and other early behavioral psychologists. They demonstrated that behaviors do not occur in a vacuum but in a lawful and predictable manner that is related directly and functionally to environmental events. Beginning with the 1968 publication of Baer, Wolf, and Risley's seminal article "Current Dimensions of Applied Behavior Analysis" in the *Journal of Applied Behavior Analysis*, the behavior analytic approach has grown to be an important means of improving behavioral outcomes for individuals with disabilities. A significant body of research has demonstrated the effectiveness and utility of a functional analytic approach, especially for individuals with developmental disabilities (Blakeslee, Sugai, & Gruba, 1994; Carr et al., 1999). In recent years, the application and usefulness of functional assessment-based behavior support

Requests for reprints should be sent to George Sugai, 5262 University of Oregon, Eugene, OR 97403–5262. E-mail: sugai@oregon.uoregon.edu

planning (BSP) have been extended to a range of individuals, including those with attention deficit hyperactivity disorder and emotional and behavioral disorders as well as those without specified disabilities (Broussard & Northup, 1995; Dunlap, White, Vera, Wilson, & Panacek, 1996; Kern, Childs, Dunlap, Clarke, & Falke, 1994; Lewis & Sugai, 1993; Lewis-Palmer, 1998; Sasso et al., 1992; Umbreit, 1995).

IDEA 1997 has heightened attention on the FBA process; however, two challenges to the implementation of the functional approach must be addressed. First, the amendments do not give practitioners who are unfamiliar with the developmental history and research base of FBA specific information about what FBA is and what the FBA process looks like. Second, some individuals who might have a basic knowledge about the FBA process lack experience and fluency with the actual implementation process. They are inefficient and ineffective in (a) applying the FBA process to a full range of problem behaviors, (b) managing the process with a large number of students, (c) collecting and using data to assess and modify ineffective interventions, (d) teaching others about the process, (e) clarifying the difference between best practice and policy, (f) sustaining accurate implementation of the FBA process for and across individuals, or a combination of these.

To address and precorrect for these challenges, this article provides an overview of the FBA process. This article is organized around "frequently asked questions." Responses to the questions include general guidelines for completing the FBA process. Brief descriptions of the necessary components required to implement the FBA process within a school also are presented. Our focus is on completing the FBA. For information about building comprehensive behavior support plans, see Horner, Sugai, Todd, and Lewis-Palmer (1999–2000/this issue).

WHAT IS FBA?

Functional behavioral assessment is a systematic *process* for understanding problem behavior and the factors that contribute to its occurrence and maintenance (Horner, 1994; O'Neill et al., 1997; Repp, 1994; Sugai et al., 2000). More important, information collected during the FBA process serves as the basis for developing individualized and comprehensive behavior intervention plans (BIP). By identifying the behavior and the context in which the behavior occurs, the efficiency and effectiveness of the subsequent BIP is increased (Horner, 1994; O'Neill et al., 1997; Sugai, Horner, & Sprague, 1999; Sugai, Lewis-Palmer, & Hagan, 1998). The FBA process should be viewed as a problem-solving strategy that consists of problem identification, information collection and analysis, intervention planning, and monitoring and evaluation.

A major outcome of the FBA process is a summary or hypothesis statement that describes the problem behaviors and the factors that are believed to be associated with occurrence and nonoccurrence of the problem behavior. Thus, whenever FBA information is being collected, the goal of developing a summary statement always should be maintained and emphasized. A complete summary statement is composed of four key components: (a) identifying the problem behavior (e.g., verbal aggression, profanity, noncompliance), (b) triggering antecedents or events that predict when the behavior is likely to occur (e.g., request to complete difficult tasks, peer teasing), (c) maintaining consequences or events that increase the likelihood of the behavior happening in the future (e.g., avoid difficult tasks, gain peer attention), and (d) setting events or factors that make the problem behavior worse (e.g., lack of peer contact in previous 30 min, missed breakfast).

Accessing problem behaviors, triggering antecedents, and maintaining consequences is relatively easy (e.g., interviews, direct observations); however, the identification of setting events can be difficult. Setting events are circumstances or factors that make the problem behavior worse (more likely to occur or be more intense) by temporarily changing the value of typical consequence events. For example, when a student has a painful ear infection, the reinforcement value of verbal praise and high grades decreases, the corrective power of simple verbal reprimands decreases, and the value of avoiding adult attention increases. Other examples of setting events include fatigue, hunger, social conflict, routine change, academic failure, and so forth.

WHY DO AN FBA?

The primary purpose of completing an FBA is to enhance the effectiveness, efficiency, and relevance of BIPs (Horner, 1994; O'Neill et al., 1997; Repp, 1994; Sugai et al., 1999). The information collected and summarized during the FBA provides the basis for selecting specific and individualized strategies and supports for a student. More important, FBA information also guides the development of scripts and procedures for adults who will implement the BIP. Clearly, the impact of the BIP on student behavior is related directly to the accuracy with which the BIP is implemented.

Although FBA information can be collected in multiple ways (e.g., interviews, ratings, direct observation), it is essential to remember that the main reason we conduct FBAs is to improve our understanding of the problem behavior and guide the development of effective, efficient, and relevant BIPs. At present, we do not have the research base that enables us to use FBAs to determine directly (a) special education eligibility, (b) placement, or (c) whether a problem behavior is a manifestation of a disability. However, FBA information may be used to guide and inform regarding these decisions. For example, a change of placement might be recommended because the current environment lacks the supports and resources to implement the BIP.

WHO DOES AN FBA?

As a process, the FBA is conducted by a team of individuals who have (a) direct experience with the student (e.g., teachers, family members, counselors); (b) behavioral expertise to lead the FBA process, collect FBA information, recommend strategies for the BIP, and so on (e.g., school psychologists, school counselors, special educators); and (c) administrative authority to support and make recommendations regarding personnel, resources, time, and so on. To the greatest degree possible, the student also should be involved.

At least one individual on the team must have the behavioral competence and expertise to lead the FBA process from problem identification, through information collection and analysis, to intervention implementation and monitoring. In addition, this person must have a working knowledge and fluency with the full range of BIP strategies for (a) minimizing, preventing, or neutralizing the impact of setting events; (b) removing antecedent events that trigger problem behavior and adding prompts that occasion appropriate behaviors; (c) teaching appropriate replacement behaviors (e.g., self-management, social skills, adaptive responses); and (d) removing consequent events that maintain problem behavior (e.g., extinction, DRO) and adding reinforcers that encourage appropriate behavior (e.g., positive reinforcement).

In sum, this individual is responsible for facilitating the team process, designing the assessment, summarizing the findings, and guiding the development of the support plan. Typically, the FBA process is led by school psychologists, school counselors, administrators, special educators, or a combination of these. However, any staff person can lead the process as long as he or she has the behavioral capacity and experience with the FBA process.

WHEN SHOULD AN FBA BE DONE?

From a "best" or "preferred" practices perspective, FBAs should be completed whenever a problem behavior is difficult to understand or a behavior intervention plan is needed to increase student success. Although the general FBA problem-solving process is basically the same across problem types, the intensity and complexity of individual FBA activities will vary; that is, not all problem behaviors and situations will require the same level of activity. For example, a teacher notices that every time Morrey makes noises in class, his peers tell him to be quiet, and then an argument occurs. Having seen Morrey engage in these behaviors a number of times, the teacher concludes that Morrey makes noises in class to access peer attention. Therefore, the teacher tells students to ignore Morrey's noises, teaches Morrey how to access peer attention in more appropriate ways, and provides positive reinforcers whenever he uses more appropriate behaviors. Basically, the teacher has assessed the situation from a functional perspective and has developed an intervention based on this assessment. In contrast, another teacher cannot figure out what triggers Leslie's temper tantrum episodes in which she throws her books, slaps her hands against the floors and walls, and screams out the windows; previous intervention attempts have produced little improvement. Therefore, to improve her understanding of the problem and modify the currently unsuccessful BIP, Leslie's teacher asks the school psychologist to interview Leslie; conduct direct observations in three periods each day for 2 days; review Leslie's educational file; and lead a BSP meeting with Leslie's dad, counselor, physical education teacher, and special education teacher. In both of these examples, problem behavior is identified, information is collected and analyzed, and an intervention is developed based on the assessment information. What varies is the intensity and complexity of the process.

In general, a two-level FBA approach should be considered (see Figure 1). At the preliminary level, the objective is to collect the smallest amount of useful information that results in summary statements to which key individuals can agree and have high confidence about their accuracy. Information might be collected through brief interviews, archival review of discipline incidents, or informal direct observations. If high agreement

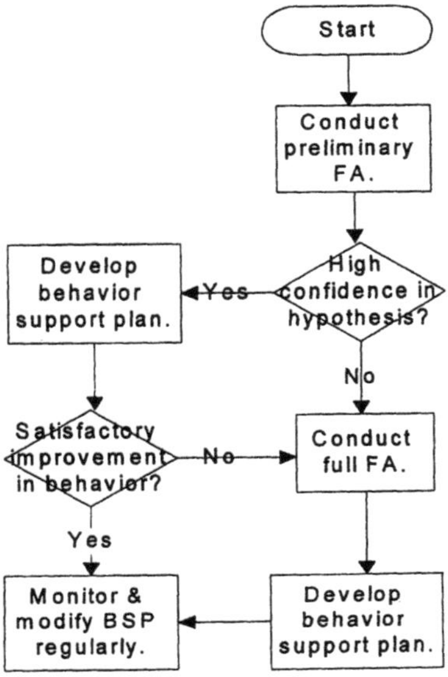

FIGURE 1 Overview of the functional behavior process. FA = functional assessment; BSP = behavior support planning.

and confidence is confirmed, then the next step is to develop and implement a behavior support plan based on that summary statement. If the plan is associated with acceptable outcomes, then the implementation and impact of the plan are monitored.

If, however, individuals do not agree with the summary statements, or lack confidence in the accuracy of the statements, the second level consists of a full FBA. Unlike the first level where information collection was informal and less intense, a team might recommend more than one type of interview (e.g., teacher, student, parent), a more thorough archival review (e.g., previous intervention plans), more formal direct observations across multiple settings (where problem behavior occurs and does not occur), or a combination of these. The additional information collected through full FBAs would be used to clarify, refine, or develop new summary statements, BIPs, or both. As with preliminary FBAs, the objective of full FBA would be to establish agreement and confidence in summary statements and develop or modify BIPs that are more likely to be effective, efficient, and relevant.

Both levels of assessment result in complete hypothesis statements and behavior support plans. They differ in the amount of information that is collected and the intensity of the assessment strategies. The general rule is that the intensity of the assessment should be matched to intensity of the problem behavior.

WHAT IS REQUIRED TO SUPPORT AND SUSTAIN THE EFFECTIVE AND EFFICIENT USE OF FBA IN SCHOOLS?

Simply having an individual within the school who has the behavioral knowledge and competence to complete and develop FBA-based BIPs is necessary but insufficient. For the FBA process to be efficient, effective, and sustained, a school environment must be established that supports all school staff in their implementation efforts. FBA-based BSP is part of a continuum of support that begins with school-wide and classroom management systems for all students, staff, and settings to specialized group-based and individualized interventions for students who display significant problem behavior. Several key components are necessary for a school to establish a full continuum of support that, in turn, supports the FBA process:

- Behavior must be considered within the *context* in which it is observed.
- *Intensity* of behavior support plans must be matched to intensity of problem behavior.
- Intervention decisions must be *data based.*
- Staff must receive *continuous feedback* on their implementation of behavior intervention plans.
- Effective *school-wide system* of behavior support must be in place.
- The adoption and sustained use of *research-validated practices* must be emphasized.
- *Behavioral competence* should be locally based (inside the school).

WHAT ARE THE MAIN STEPS IN THE FBA PROCESS?

Although variations exist based on the intensity of the problem behavior, the main steps of the FBA process are basically the same. The FBA process is composed of the following seven main steps.

Collect Information

To build summary statements that describe the problem behavior and the context in which it is observed, information is collected via interviews, ratings, archival reviews, and informal direct observations. How the information is collected is determined by a team of individuals (e.g., teachers, administrators, counselors, family members) who have direct experience with the student and know him or her well.

Develop Summary Statement

Information collected in the first step is used to develop summary or hypothesis statements that describe the problem behavior and the context in which it is observed. Complete summary statements are composed of four components: problem behavior, triggering antecedent, maintaining consequences, and setting events. See Figure 2 for an example.

Collect Direct Observation Data to Confirm Summary Statement

Once the summary statement is developed and before a support plan is developed, formal direct observation information must be collected to verify the accuracy of the summary

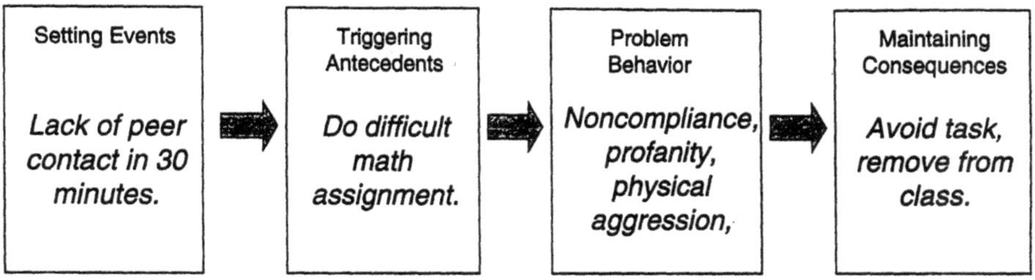

FIGURE 2 Example of summary or hypothesis statement.

statement. Direct observations should be completed across multiple settings, days, times, and activities and should include measures of problem behavior, triggering antecedents, maintaining consequences, and the influence of setting events.

Develop "Competing Pathways" Summary Statement

The competing pathway summary extends the confirmed summary statement by identifying (a) a *desired* replacement behavior to be displayed in the problem situation (behavioral objective), (b) an *alternative* replacement behavior that functions like the problem behavior but is more acceptable or appropriate than the problem behavior, and (c) the *consequences* that are naturally available or normally provided to support the occurrence of the desired replacement behaviors. See Figure 3.

Develop Behavior Support Plan

Based on the features of the competing pathways summary, an individualized, comprehensive, and multicomponent support plan is developed. The support plan focuses on the identification of strategies for (a) teaching the desired and alternative replacement behaviors to compete with occurrences of problem behavior, (b) manipulating antecedent events that decrease the likelihood of problem behavior and increase the probability of desired and alternative replacement behaviors, (c) manipulating consequence events to discourage problem behavior (e.g., extinction, DRO) and encourage desired and alternative replacement behaviors (i.e., positive reinforcement), and (d) eliminating setting events or neutralizing the impact of setting events. In addition, the plan includes descriptions of procedures for preventing and responding to emergency or crisis situations and monitoring the implementation effectiveness and impact.

Develop Details and Routines for Full Implementation of Behavior Support Plan

After the components of the plan have been identified, the specific procedures for implementation of the plan components are determined. Emphasis is placed on specification of

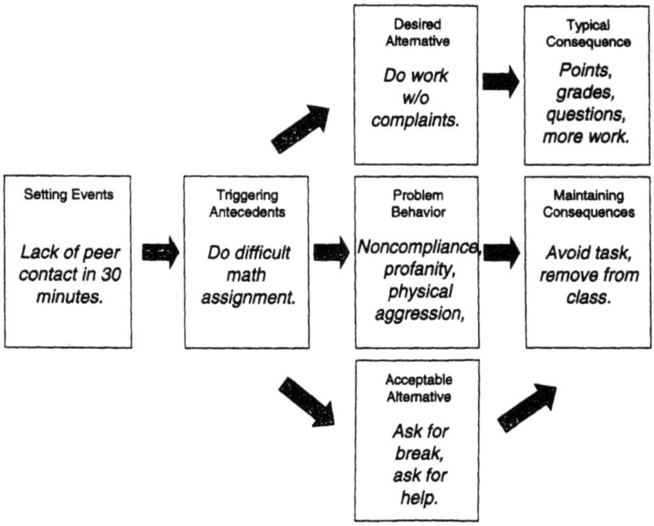

FIGURE 3 Example of a competing pathways summary.

the adult behaviors, routines, and sequences that will ensure accurate and consistent implementation of the plan. The team considers logistics (e.g., schedules, materials, training); develops scripts for key individuals to follow during implementation of the plan; and modifies routines, physical aspects of the environment, and so on.

Monitor and Evaluate Implementation of Behavior Support Plan

The final step in the FBA–BIP process is to specify strategies and data for monitoring the implementation and effectiveness of the behavior intervention plan. Specifically, data are used to evaluate the extent to which (a) the student is making satisfactory progress, (b) the intervention has an impact on lifestyle outcomes (e.g., interpersonal skills, career development, family relations), (c) individuals who know the student report satisfactory change in student behavior (social validation), and (d) the behavior intervention plan is implemented with high fidelity.

HOW DO I KNOW WHEN AN FBA HAS BEEN DONE?

As previously stated, the intensity and complexity of the FBA process implementation will vary with the intensity and complexity of the problem behavior. However, the basic steps and general process essentially remain the same. A FBA is complete when the steps described have been completed and the following outcomes are produced:

1. Summary statement including problem behavior, triggering antecedents, maintaining consequences, and setting events.
2. Data to confirm the accuracy of the summary statement.
3. Competing pathways summary.
4. Behavior support or intervention plan.
5. Implementation plan that specifies what, who, when, and how the BIP is to be implemented.
6. A monitoring plan to assess the effectiveness and implementation of the BIP.

CONCLUSIONS

The FBA technology has a long history, and its utility has been demonstrated in the empirical and applied literature. Although attention on FBA has increased with the 1997 amendments to IDEA, the purpose and essential features of the FBA process have not been emphasized. The purpose of this article was to provide an overview of the FBA process and highlight the necessary and essential features and steps of the process. The checklist illustrated in the Appendix provides a summary of these steps.

ACKNOWLEDGMENTS

This article was supported in part by U.S. Department of Education Grant No. H326S980003. The opinions expressed herein do not necessarily reflect the position or policy of the Department, and no official endorsement by the Department should be inferred.

REFERENCES

Baer, D. M., Wolf, M. M., & Risley, T. R. (1968). Some current dimensions of applied behavior analysis. *Journal of Applied Behavior Analysis, 1,* 91–97.

Blakeslee, T., Sugai, G., & Gruba, J. (1994). A review of functional assessment use in data-based intervention studies. *Journal of Behavioral Education, 4,* 397–414.

Broussard, C. D., & Northup, J. (1995). An approach to functional assessment and analysis of disruptive behavior in regular education classrooms. *School Psychology Quarterly, 10,* 151–164.

Carr, E. G., Horner, R. H., Turnbull, A. P., Marquis, J. G., McLaughlin, D. M., McAtee, M. L., Smith, C. E., Ryan, K. A., Ruef, M. B., Doolabh, A., & Braddock, D. (1999). *Positive behavior support for people with developmental disabilities: A research synthesis.* Washington, DC: American Association on Mental Retardation.

Dunlap, G., White, R., Vera, A., Wilson, D., & Panacek, L. (1996). The effects of multi- component, assessment-based curricular modifications on the classroom behavior of children with emotional and behavioral disorders. *Journal of Behavioral Education, 6,* 481–500.

Individuals With Disabilities Education Act Amendments of 1997, 20 U.S.C. § 1400 *et seq.* (1997).

Horner, R. H. (1994). Functional assessment: Contributions and future directions. *Journal of Applied Behavior Analysis, 27,* 401–404.

Horner, R. H., Sugai, G., Todd, A. W., & Lewis-Palmer, T. (1999–2000/this issue). Elements of behavior support plans: A technical brief. *Exceptionality, 8,* 205–215.

Kern, L., Childs, K. E., Dunlap, G., Clarke, S., & Falke, G. D. (1994). Using assessment-based curricular intervention to improve the classroom behaviors of a student with emotional and behavioral challenges. *Journal of Applied Behavior Analysis, 27,* 7–19.

Lewis, T. J., & Sugai, G. (1993). Functional assessment of problem behavior: A pilot investigation of the comparative and interactive effects of teacher and peer social attention on students in general education settings. *School Psychology Quarterly, 11*(1), 1–19.

Lewis-Palmer, T. (1998). *Using functional assessment strategies in regular classroom settings with students at-risk for school failure.* Unpublished doctoral dissertation, University of Oregon, Eugene.

O'Neill, R. E., Horner, R. H., Albin, R. W., Sprague, J. R., Storey, K., & Newton, J. S. (1997). *Functional assessment and program development for problem behavior: A practical handbook* (2nd ed.). Pacific Grove, CA: Brooks/Cole.

Repp, A. C. (1994). Comments on functional analysis procedures for school-based behavior problems. *Journal of Applied Behavior Analysis, 27,* 409–411.

Sasso, G. M., Reimers, T. M., Cooper, L. J., Wacker, D., Berg, W., Steege, M., Kelly, L., & Allaire, A. (1992). Use of descriptive and experimental analyses to identify the functional properties of aberrant behavior in school settings. *Journal of Applied Behavior Analysis, 25,* 809–821.

Sugai, G., Horner, R. H., Dunlap, G., Hieneman, M., Lewis, T. J., Nelson, C. M., Scott, T., Liaupsin, C., Sailor, W., Turnbull, A. P., Turnbull, H. R., III, Wickham, D., Reuf, M., & Wilcox, B. (2000). Applying positive behavioral support and functional behavioral assessment in schools. *Journal of Positive Behavioral Interventions and Support, 2,* 131–143.

Sugai, G., Horner, R. H., & Sprague, J. (1999). Functional assessment-based behavior support planning: Research-to-practice-to-research. *Behavioral Disorders, 24,* 223–227.

Sugai, G., Lewis-Palmer, T., & Hagan, S. (1998). Using functional assessments to develop behavior support plans. *Preventing School Failure, 43*(1), 6–13.

Umbreit, J. (1995). Functional assessment and intervention in a regular classroom setting for the disruptive behavior of a student with attention deficit hyperactivity disorder. *Behavioral Disorders, 20,* 267–278.

APPENDIX

FBA Implementation Checklist

Student ____________

Date ________

When completing an FBA, ensure that all steps have been completed. For items marked "Y" (yes), go to the next step or activity. For items marked "N" (no), review activity or go back to previous step or activity.

Step	*Activity*	*Status*	*Action Plan*
1. Collect information.	1. Include key individuals in the initial assessment meetings.	Y N	
	2. Review relevant records.	Y N	
	3. Collect informal direct observation data.	Y N	
	4. Interview individuals who have direct experience with the student.	Y N	
2. Develop summary statement.	1. Define problem behavior in observable terms.	Y N	
	2. Identify triggering antecedent events.	Y N	
	3. Identify maintaining consequence events.	Y N	
	4. Identify possible setting events.	Y N	
	5. Develop summary statements based on Activities 1–4.	Y N	
	6. Determine level of agreement or confidence that individuals have in resulting summary statement.	Y N	If agreement or confidence is high, go to Step 3. If low, go back to Step 1.
3. Confirm summary statement.	1. Collect formal direct observation information on behavior, antecedents, and consequences.	Y N	
	2. Determine if direct observation data confirm summary statement.	Y N	If summary statement is confirmed, go to Step 4. If not confirmed, go back to Step 2.
4. Develop competing behavior pathway summary.	1. Identify desired replacement behavior (long-term objective).	Y N	
	2. Identify common reinforcing consequences for desired replacement behavior.	Y N	
	3. Identify alternative replacement behavior(s) based on function of problem behavior (short-term objectives).	Y N	

(Continued)

APPENDIX (Continued)

Step	*Activity*	*Status*	*Action Plan*
	4. Determine level of agreement or confidence in competing pathway summary.	Y N	If agreement or confidence is high, got to Step 5. If low, repeat Step 4.
5. Identify strategies for BIP.	1. Select strategies, environmental manipulations, or both that neutralize impact of setting events.	Y N	
	2. Select strategies, environmental manipulations, or both that make triggering antecedents irrelevant.	Y N	
	3. Select strategies, environmental manipulations, or both that teach student skills that make problem behavior inefficient.	Y N	
	4. Select strategies, environmental manipulations, or both that make consequences for problem behavior ineffective.	Y N	
	5. If necessary, develop additional (beyond current school-wide) crisis prevention and intervention procedures.	Y N	
6. Develop implementation scripts for BIP.	1. Develop scripts and routines for implementation of BIP.	Y N	
	2. Identify who will implement BIP.	Y N	
	3. Determine if resources and capacity to implement BIP are available.	Y N	If capacity is adequate, implement. If inadequate, obtain resources, modify context, or adjust implementation requirements.
7. Develop evaluation and monitoring procedures.	1. Identify measures to assess impact: (a) target behaviors, (b) social validation, (c) lifestyle, and so on.	Y N	
	2. Develop schedule for ongoing evaluation of implementation impact.	Y N	
	3. Develop procedures for assessing accuracy of BIP implementation.	Y N	
	4. Assess progress toward achieving long-term objective.	Y N	If adequate, continue. If criteria met, develop new objective. If inadequate, go back to Step 1.

Note. FBA = functional behavioral assessment. BIP = behavior intervention plan.

EXCEPTIONALITY, *8*(3), 161–172

Contextual, Conceptual, and Empirical Foundations of Functional Behavioral Assessment in Schools

Deanne A. Crone and Robert H. Horner
Special Education Area
University of Oregon

This article examines the contextual, conceptual, and empirical foundations of functional behavioral assessment (FBA) in general educational settings. Schools today face 2 important, contextual challenges: the need to design effective responses to increases in individual problem behavior and the need to be compliant with the 1997 amendments to the Individuals With Disabilities Education Act. FBA as a solution to these challenges is explored from a conceptual framework. Finally, the empirical literature supporting the use of FBA in typical school settings is reviewed briefly.

The field of functional behavioral assessment (FBA) is evolving—from a methodology implemented primarily with individuals with severe developmental disabilities to a system of recommended practice in schools. The increased demand for FBA in schools results from at least two contextual factors: (a) existing approaches to problem behavior in schools are no longer seen as adequate, and (b) there is a discrepancy between legislative mandates and the skills, resources, and training currently available in schools. This section describes these two factors and considers the parameters needed for embedding FBA within schools' systems of behavior support.

CONTEXT 1: INADEQUATE APPROACH TO PROBLEM BEHAVIOR

Impact of Problem Behavior in Schools

The primary purpose of schools is to educate children. Yet, one of the biggest problems faced by public schools is not related to curriculum, instruction, or even learning difficulties. Safety and discipline are part of the nation's primary goals for education (U.S. De-

Requests for reprints should be sent to Deanne A. Crone, 5208 University of Oregon, Eugene, OR 97403. E-mail: dcrone@oregon.uoregon.edu

partment of Education, 1999). Even so, four of the five areas of significant decline in national educational performance were related to National Educational Goal 7, "Safe, Disciplined, and Alcohol- and Drug-Free Schools." Individual problem behavior affects everyone involved in schools.

A significant portion of an administrator's time is spent dealing with the problem behavior of a few students, completing related paperwork, and responding to unhappy parents and teachers. Sugai and Horner (1999) found that 40.4% of the referrals in nine middle schools were accounted for by 5% of the students. Responding to the behavioral referrals these students generate can consume much of the school personnel's resources and attention.

Individual problem behavior is burdensome to teachers. Problem behavior reduces the teacher's ability to provide effective instruction to the individual student and the student's classmates. Many teachers—even special education teachers—do not have training in effective behavior management, leaving them feeling powerless and ineffective in the face of problem behavior. For example, in a survey of 157 teachers of students with severe disabilities, 82% said they felt that the current resources available to them were inadequate for meeting the needs of their students with serious problem behaviors (Horner, Diemer, & Brazeau, 1992).

Problem behavior has a serious negative impact on the individual students. Students demonstrating serious or persistent problem behaviors are more likely to engage in criminal or harmful, antisocial behaviors (Walker, Colvin, & Ramsey, 1995). If not identified early, these children are at a higher risk for experiencing academic failure and developing severe noncompliance, aggression, or even delinquency (Walker et al., 1995).

Finally, individual problem behavior in schools has begun to affect the larger community. Extremely violent incidents in school have become the focus of increasing media attention (e.g., the shootings at Thurston High School in Oregon and Columbine High School in Colorado). Correspondingly, the demand from parents and the community to increase school safety, deal effectively with problem behavior, and respond proactively to warning signs of problem behavior has also increased.

A Common Response to Problem Behavior

A common view taken by school personnel is that problem behavior is unpredictable and driven by within-child pathology (e.g., ascribing the child's problem behavior to a diagnosis of attention deficit hyperactivity disorder [ADHD] or fetal alcohol syndrome). One outcome of this view is that responses to behavior are reactive, not proactive, and interventions are topological, not individualized.

Schools traditionally have relied on punishment-based approaches to behavior control such as detention and suspension. For example, in a survey of 371 elementary, junior high, and high schools, 67.5% of the principals responded that they routinely use in-school suspension as a discipline practice. In addition, 80.6% of principals indicated that they regularly use out-of-school suspension, and 44.7% indicated that they use expulsion as part of their discipline response (Rose, 1988). Costenbader and Markson (1998) discussed several studies that indicate these short-term solutions do not result in long-term reduction of problem behavior, generalization of behavior change, or acquisition of appropriate replacement behaviors.

Problem behavior compromises schools' basic ability to provide an education to all students. Teachers, parents, schools, and communities are frustrated. They want classrooms to be places of learning, not battlegrounds for misbehavior. Yet, schools often lack the tools for identifying effective solutions to behavior problems.

This contextual factor illustrates the clear need to identify and implement an effective system of behavior assessment and intervention in schools.

CONTEXT 2: DISCREPANCY BETWEEN LEGISLATIVE DEMANDS AND AVAILABLE RESOURCES

Congress has recognized the impact that serious behavior problems might have on a child's academic, social, and family functioning. The amendments to the Individuals With Disabilities Education Act (IDEA; 1997) explicitly recommend that schools use FBA procedures to develop intervention strategies for children with disabilities who display severe behavior problems. A functional assessment of behavior is required before a school suspends (for more than 10 days in 1 academic year) or expels a student with a disability (IDEA, 1997). The article by Wilcox, Turnbull, and Turnbull (1999–2000/this issue) delineates the implication of this legislative policy for schools.

In the past, serious behavior problems have been the concern of psychiatrists and probation officers. The recent legislative measures have shifted much of the responsibility for managing problem behavior onto administrators, teachers, and other school staff (IDEA, 1997). For many educators, these are unfamiliar roles. As a result, many school personnel are under pressure to provide effective services in FBA and intervention without the requisite knowledge, training, or resources to carry out this mandate.

The discrepancy between legislative mandates and available resources has created an unusual circumstance for researchers in the field of FBA: (a) Public schools (typically hesitant to implement innovative, systems-wide prevention efforts) are requesting training in FBA, and (b) legislative policy that is driving the demand for training and implementation has come before a large body of evidence has accumulated to support the legitimacy of its use in the general education setting (Nelson, Roberts, Mathur, & Rutherford, 1999).

This context lays the foundation for training and further research in FBA and increases the likelihood that FBA will become an integral part of schools' responses to individual problem behavior.

EMBEDDING FBA WITHIN THE CONTEXTUAL PARAMETERS OF THE SCHOOL

In schools, problem behavior must be addressed at multiple levels. The culture of every school is comprised of multiple systems—the school-wide system, the classroom system, specific settings systems (e.g., cafeteria, hallways), and individual systems. Problem behavior can occur within each of these systems and can impact the occurrence of problem behavior within each of the other systems.

FBA and behavior support typically address problem behavior only at the level of the individual. To understand how this level of behavior support fits within the broader systems of the entire school, it is essential to consider two points: (a) Problem behavior is not always generated by individual factors, and behavioral interventions should not always be targeted to individuals. A systems-based approach to behavior support examines the entire context of the school and determines where to leverage the intervention to get the most impact for the least effort. (b) Problem behavior that originates in a larger system (e.g., cafeteria, classroom) can increase the likelihood that an individual will engage in problem behavior. This underscores the need to look at alterable, environmental (systems-level) events in designing interventions to change behavior.

Need

These three issues (inadequate approach to problem behavior, discrepancy between legislative demands and available resources, and systems-wide approach to behavior support) describe the context of today's schools and define their needs relevant to FBA. Schools need a technology that will effectively reduce the negative impact of problem behavior, can be used by school staff, and can be implemented efficiently by pairing resources to problems at the appropriate system level. The immediate challenge is to respond to these contextual demands by transforming legislative policy into an accessible methodology that can be applied in typical educational settings. The next section addresses conceptual aspects of FBA that demonstrate how FBA can respond to this challenge.

CONCEPTUAL FOUNDATIONS

Responding to Context 1: Inadequate Approach to Problem Behavior

For many schools, the emphasis on functional assessment of problem behaviors represents a dramatic shift in philosophy. Four conceptual foundations of the FBA approach illustrate this difference: (a) Behavior is viewed as predictable and changeable rather than unpredictable and recalcitrant; (b) focus of intervention and treatment is on alterable, environmental events that contribute to problem behavior rather than within-child pathology; (c) intervention strategies are preventive and proactive with an emphasis on positive behavior substitution rather than reactive and punishing, and (d) intervention is individualized to match the antecedents, behaviors, consequences, and functions of the specific problem behavior rather than matching the intervention to the topology of the behavior. A successful system of individual behavior support must be effective, efficient, and relevant. The following section demonstrates how the four conceptual foundations of FBA meet these criteria.

Behavior Is Predictable and Supported by Alterable Environmental Events

Many school personnel view problem behaviors as unpredictable events originating within the individual, not as predictable events influenced by environmental constraints. Children engage in problem behavior because they are "troublemakers," "wired that way," or have some type of "disorder," and not because "there is something about the child's environment that is triggering and maintaining problem behavior." When problem behavior is viewed as both unpredictable and trait based, school personnel who have been charged with reducing the impact of problem behavior on teachers, students, and communities might feel frustrated and overwhelmed.

FBA is based on a much different conceptual understanding of behavior. FBA is a process of looking for alterable variables in the environment that set up, set off, or maintain problem behavior (i.e., setting events, antecedents, and consequences; O'Neill et al., 1997). A basic tenet of FBA is that people act the way they do for a reason (O'Neill et al., 1997). Most behavior is functional; it serves a purpose. Engaging in different behaviors might help individuals obtain something they want or escape something aversive. By identifying biological, social, affective, or environmental factors that initiate and maintain the problem behavior, it becomes possible to understand the student's underlying motivation. Understanding the functions, predictors, and consequences of problem behavior helps to pinpoint and script effective behavioral interventions (e.g., Umbreit, 1995).

Intervention Should Be Individualized, Not Based on the Topology of Behavior

Individual variability in response to treatment is perhaps the most difficult challenge in intervening with children with behavior problems. Rather than maximizing the match between the individual student's needs and the chosen intervention strategy, behavior intervention plans often are based on whatever strategy or combination of strategies the interventionist has used previously to reduce the occurrence of a particular type of problem behavior. As a result, all children exhibiting the same type of behavior problems (e.g., disruption, noncompliance, inattention) might receive the same intervention. FBA takes a less generic approach and considers the unique features of the situation, child, or behavior that predict the success or failure of a behavioral intervention.

A focus on the individual, rather than on the topology of the behavior, leads to an intervention that is more relevant to the student. To illustrate, consider the following example. A middle school identifies a group of students who are at risk for chronic problem behaviors (disruption, noncompliance, inattention, etc.). The school personnel implement a targeted group intervention for these students. Each student is given a behavior card that outlines common behavioral goals for the day (e.g., "arrive to class on time and with all necessary materials," "keep hands and feet to self"). Every morning, the students check in with an educational assistant. The students pick up a new behavior card for the day and receive encouragement and reinforcement from the aide. Throughout the day, the teachers of each student rate (on a scale of 0–2 ranging from 0 [*did not meet expectations*] to 2 [*consistently met expectations*]) the extent to which the student has met the behavioral goals. At the end of the day, the students check out with the educational assistant, turning in a copy of their behavior card and bringing home a second copy for the students' parents to review and sign.

This approach to behavior change is very effective for some students and ineffective or even detrimental for other students. It is very likely that the difference lies in the function of the problem behavior. For a student who is being disruptive and noncompliant to gain attention, the targeted group intervention should be very effective. It shifts the adult's response to provide attention for appropriate, not inappropriate, behavior. However, for a student whose problem behavior is driven by a desire to escape interaction with adults, the intervention is likely to worsen or increase their problem behavior.

Intervention Should Be Proactive and Preventive, Not Reactive

The most common responses to individual problem behavior in schools are also some of the most inefficient approaches. Reactive, punishment-based procedures such as detention, suspension, or expulsion require the student to misbehave before receiving an adult response. These discipline strategies frequently are ineffective in preventing future problem behavior. For example, Costenbader and Markson (1998) surveyed 620 middle and high school students on the topic of suspension. Of the students who had received out-of-school suspension, 33% stated that they felt suspension was "not at all" helpful and that they would "probably be suspended again." In a separate question, 31% of students indicated that they were "happy to get out of the situation" (that had gotten them suspended in the first place).

In contrast, FBA is a proactive, preventive approach. One purpose of FBA is to help school personnel predict patterns of problem behavior and identify strategies to reduce the likelihood that problem behavior will continue to occur. Prevention of future problem behavior can be achieved in at least two ways: First, the student is taught appropriate replacement behaviors. For example, a student who consistently bullies other students to be included in a game at recess can be taught how to ask for his turn to play. Second, the teacher is taught to manipulate antecedents. For example, a teacher might expect third-grade students to not talk to each other during class but still group their desks into pods of four, facing each other. This physical arrangement is sure to set up and increase the likelihood that students will talk to each other and be off task. By rearranging the physical arrangement of the classroom (i.e., manipulating antecedents), the teacher can reduce the occurrence of talk-outs in class. Through an emphasis on prevention, FBA leads to a response that is more efficient in reducing problem behavior.

Responding to Context 2: Discrepancy Between Legislation and Resources

Schools face legislative mandates to conduct FBA in certain circumstances (IDEA, 1997). Currently, many schools do not have the necessary resources or skills to conduct these assessments. This discrepancy between legislative demands and existing resources creates a need to develop the resources within the school. This section outlines three key features of our conceptual model for embedding a system of FBA-based behavior support planning (BSP) in schools: (a) FBA–BSP should be team based, (b) each member of the team must be skilled in FBA–BSP, and (c) the school must provide the necessary support to sustain and maintain the team.

Team Based

Two basic principles underlie our model for a school's system for embedding a function-based approach to individual behavior support. First, an effective system of individual behavior support benefits from a team-based approach (Todd, Horner, Sugai, & Colvin, 1999). An individual behavior support system that relies on one person is not desirable or sustainable. The loss of one individual to a new job, illness, or maternity leave should not result in the loss of the school's entire system of individual behavior support. Second, the team structure should be able to support a dynamic membership. Schools seem to be in a continual state of flux, and it is not always possible to predict staff responsibilities from year to year. By developing within-building capacity in behavioral assessment and intervention skills, the individual behavior support system can become resilient to inconstant team membership.

It is important to have an administrator and an individual with expertise in behavioral assessment and intervention serve on the team (Todd et al., 1999). In addition, the team might consist of a general education teacher, special education teacher, educational assistant, or school counselor. Each of these team members will bring different perspectives to bear on an individual referral, and the team will benefit from the combined strengths of their multiple skills and abilities.

All teams should share certain defining features and objectives. Todd et al. (1999) outlined these features:

> Teams that support students with chronic problem behaviors need to (a) possess specialized behavioral skills within its membership, (b) allow and encourage contributions from all its members, (c) have predictable and efficient procedures for doing business and solving problems, [and] (d) have regular opportunities to access building staff, families and community agencies to communicate and solicit information. (p. 74)

A team that possesses these defining features should be able to meet the following primary objectives:

> (a) manage teacher requests for assistance, (b) ensure that teachers and students receive support in a timely and meaningful manner, (c) provide a general forum for discussions and possible solutions for individual student behavioral concerns, and (d) organize a collaborative effort to support the teacher. (p. 74)

Skilled Team Members

Skill development and sustainability are two important issues to consider in developing, implementing, and embedding a system of FBA–BSP within a school. Skill development can occur through a sequence of training, modeling, practicing, and feedback. Leighton et al. (1997) identified several activities that should be applied in effective training, including: "(a) formal orientation that sets the foundation for the individual's work, (b) training sessions that supplement and enhance knowledge and skill development, and (c) structured, on-the-job coaching in classrooms or other learning environments" (pp. v–vi). The behavior team leader or team trainer should teach the necessary content knowledge, model the necessary skills, provide multiple opportunities to practice, and give formative constructive feedback that leads to progressive improvement and mastery.

Support From School

To ensure implementation and sustainability of a system of individual behavioral support, the school must provide adequate support. In our model, the critical features schools should agree to include (a) commitment to behavior support as a top-three priority goal, (b) coordination of a team and a process, (c) administrative support, (d) adequate allocation of financial resources and time resources, and (e) development of behavioral competence in staff members (Todd et al., 1999).

EMPIRICAL FOUNDATIONS

Empirical Background and History of FBA: A Maturing Technology

Increased Efficiency of Procedures

FBA typically has been characterized by procedures that require very skilled personnel and considerable periods of time, thus limiting their use. According to Schill, Kratochwill, and Elliott (1998), the amount of time required to complete the FBA–BSP process ranged from 9.7 to 23 consultant hours, with a mean of 14.7 hr. If FBA is to become a basic tool within schools, the efficiency of the procedures must be improved, both in terms of who can use them and the amount of time required. As noted by Horner (1994), "the major difficulty comes from trying to identify a procedure that both delivers very precise, usable, valid information about the problem behavior, yet does so with minimal time, effort, and expectations about the skills of the implementers" (p. 402).

Changing population. In a review of 97 studies on FBA, Nelson et al. (1999) noted that the majority (88%) of participants had low-incidence disabilities (e.g., severe mental retardation). Only 23% of the studies were conducted in school settings, whereas 63% were conducted in clinical settings. Although FBA procedures have been in use for over 30 years, only recently has FBA been used or recommended for use in general education settings with general education students.

Some researchers have questioned the amendments to IDEA 1997, demonstrating that the new legislative policy has come before an adequate body of empirical evidence supporting the use of FBA–BSP in general education settings (Nelson et al., 1999).

These researchers question the wisdom of mandating FBA for conditions so far removed from the empirically documented uses of this procedure.

These researchers raise a valid concern while underscoring an inherent paradox. An obligation exists to fulfill an immediate training need. An equally or more important obligation exists to empirically test the validity and effectiveness of training on student behavior and teacher behavior. Researchers in the fields of special education and school psychology have begun to address both of these needs (e.g., Broussard & Northrup, 1995; Chandler, Dahlquist, Repp, & Feltz, 1999; Ervin, DuPaul, Kern, & Friman, 1998; Northrup et al., 1994; Umbreit, 1995).

EMPIRICAL EVIDENCE: CURRENT LITERATURE

Application in General Education Settings

Recent empirical evidence does suggest that FBA can be an effective tool in changing the problem behavior of students without developmental disabilities or students in general education settings (e.g., Broussard & Northrup, 1995; Ervin et al., 1998; Umbreit, 1995). These initial studies suggest that recent innovations, legal mandates, or changes in educational philosophy have increased the efficiency of FBA procedures, extended the range of professionals who can contribute to FBA, extended the use of FBA to a larger population of students, or generalized the application of FBA to students in general education settings (e.g., Broussard & Northrup, 1995; Ellingson, Miltenberger, Stricker, Galensky, & Garlinghouse, 2000; Ervin et al., 1998; Lewis & Sugai, 1996; Umbreit, 1995).

Lewis and Sugai (1996) conducted one of the first studies to bridge the gap between students in general education settings and the use of functional assessment procedures originally developed for individuals with developmental delays in nontraditional settings. These researchers examined the disruptive behaviors of a 7-year-old boy and two 9-year-old boys. One of the boys was diagnosed with ADHD the year following his participation in the study. All three children engaged in off-task behavior and inappropriate peer interactions. Two of the boys were frequently noncompliant with teacher directions. Functional assessment data were collected through teacher interview and direct observations. For each student, functional assessment data suggested that the problem behavior was functioning as a means to obtain peer or teacher attention. These hypothesis statements were confirmed through subsequent manipulations of the amount of peer or teacher attention received. Manipulation of teacher attention resulted in an increase of on-task behavior for two of the study participants.

Umbreit (1995) also examined the use of functional assessment to select school-based intervention strategies to reduce the disruptive behavior of an 8-year-old child in a general education setting. The functional assessment suggested that the function of the problem behavior was to escape from task demands. Furthermore, certain seating arrangements were more likely than others to produce disruptive behavior. Based on this information, an intervention was developed that included altering the student's seating arrangement and teaching him to request a break when he needed it rather than engage in disruptive behavior to escape a difficult task. These intervention strategies were successful in significantly reducing the disruptive behavior of this student. In addition to these two studies, other single-subject studies (e.g., Broussard & Northrup, 1995; Ervin et al., 1998) demonstrate the treatment utility of using functional assessment to link the function of problem behaviors of students to effective school-based interventions.

Inclusion of School Personnel in FBA–BSP Process

Multiple studies have begun to empirically test the feasibility and effectiveness of including teachers and other school personnel in the assessment and intervention planning components of FBA–BSP (e.g., Chandler et al., 1999; Ellingson et al., 2000; Northrup et al., 1994; Selinske, Greer, & Lodhi, 1991). Ellingson et al. (2000) demonstrated that teachers were able to accurately identify antecedents and consequences of problem behavior using a structured interview format. These same teachers were able to use direct observation to identify antecedents, problem behaviors, and consequences with results comparable to those found by graduate students with 2 years of experience and training in applied behavior analysis.

Northrup et al. (1994) applied a technical assistance model to train special education teachers, with no previous experience in functional analysis, to conduct functional analyses and implement interventions within the natural classroom setting. The technical assistance model consisted of a 2-day workshop (on behavioral assessment and intervention with an emphasis on functional analysis) plus frequent (half-day weekly and full day bi-weekly) on-site, student-specific consultation. Teachers were able to implement all aspects of assessment and intervention with occasional technical assistance and interventions were effective in reducing behavior problems. One problem with this study was the immoderate amount of time required in terms of consultation and assistance. An important challenge for the future will be to identify the most efficient, yet effective, model for training school-based teams to implement FBA–BSP in the general education setting.

CONCLUSIONS

This article has explored the contextual, conceptual, and empirical foundations of FBA in schools. The contextual foundations identified two areas of need and their parameters—that is, the need to change the current response to problem behavior in schools and the discrepancy between legislative demands and existing resources. The conceptual foundations explored FBA as a solution to these needs. The empirical foundations reviewed the existing literature that has evaluated the effectiveness and feasibility of FBA in schools as a solution to individual problem behavior.

Based on a small, but growing, body of empirical research, FBA in general education settings appears to be a feasible and effective solution to individual problem behavior. Further research will need to be conducted to (a) compare FBA against other methodologies of behavioral assessment and treatment, (b) test the effectiveness and sustainability of team-based training in FBA–BSP, and (c) increase the external validity and generalizability of results by building a larger body of empirical evidence for the use of FBA in general education.

ACKNOWLEDGMENTS

This article was supported in part by U.S. Department of Education Grant No. H326S980003. The opinions expressed herein do not necessarily reflect the position or policy of the Department, and no official endorsement by the Department should be inferred.

REFERENCES

Broussard, C. D., & Northrup, J. (1995). An approach to functional assessment and analysis of disruptive behavior in regular education classrooms. *School Psychology Quarterly, 10,* 151–164.

Chandler, L. K., Dahlquist, C. M., Repp, A. C., & Feltz, C. (1999). The effects of team- based functional assessment on the behavior of students in classroom settings. *Exceptional Children, 66,* 101–122.

Costenbader, V., & Markson, S. (1998). School suspension: A study with secondary school students. *Journal of School Psychology, 36,* 59–82.

Ellingson, S. A., Miltenberger, R. G., Stricker, J., Galensky, T. L., & Garlinghouse, M. (2000). Functional assessment and intervention for challenging behaviors in the classroom by general classroom teachers. *Journal of Positive Behavior Interventions, 2,* 85–97.

Ervin, R. A., DuPaul, G. J., Kern, L., & Friman, P. C. (1998). Classroom-based functional and adjunctive assessments: Proactive approaches to intervention selection for adolescents with attention deficit hyperactivity disorder. *Journal of Applied Behavior Analysis, 31,* 65–78.

Horner, R. H. (1994). Functional assessment: Contributions and future directions. *Journal of Applied Behavior Analysis, 27,* 401–404.

Horner, R. H., Diemer, S. M., & Brazeau, K. C. (1992). Educational support for students with severe problem behaviors in Oregon: A descriptive analysis from the 1987–88 school year. *Journal of the Association for Persons With Severe Handicaps, 17,* 154–169.

Individuals With Disabilities Education Act Amendments of 1997, 20 U.S.C. § 1400 *et seq.* (1997). Retrieved April 15, 2000 from the World Wide Web: http://www.ed.gov/offices/OSERS/IDEA

Leighton, M. S., O'Brien, E., Walking Eagle, K., Weiner, L., Wimberly, G., & Youngs, P. (1997). *Roles for education paraprofessionals in effective schools: An idea book.* Washington, DC: U.S. Department of Education.

Lewis, T. J., & Sugai, G. (1996). Functional assessment of problem behavior: A pilot investigation of the comparative and interactive effects of teacher and peer social attention on students in general education settings. *School Psychology Quarterly, 11,* 1–19.

Nelson, J. R., Roberts, M., Mathur, S., & Rutherford, R. B. (1999). Has public policy exceeded our knowledge base? A review of the functional assessment literature. *Behavioral Disorders, 24,* 169–179.

Northrup, J., Wacker, D. P., Berg, W. K., Kelly, L., Sasso, G., & DeRaad, A. (1994). The treatment of severe behavior problems in school settings using a technical assistance model. *Journal of Applied Behavior Analysis, 27,* 33–47.

O'Neill, R. E., Horner, R. H., Albin, R. W., Sprague, J. R., Storey, K., & Newton, J. S. (1997). *Functional assessment for problem behavior: A practical handbook* (2nd ed.). Pacific Grove, CA: Brooks/Cole.

Rose, T. L. (1988). Current disciplinary practices with handicapped students: Suspensions and expulsions. *Exceptional Children, 55,* 230–239.

Schill, M. T., Kratochwill, T. R., & Elliott, S. N. (1998). Functional assessment in behavioral consultation: A treatment utility study. *School Psychology Quarterly, 13,* 116–140.

Selinske, J. E., Greer, R. D., & Lodhi, S. (1991). A functional analysis of the comprehensive application of behavior analysis to schooling. *Journal of Applied Behavior Analysis, 24,* 107–117.

Sugai, G., & Horner, R. (1999). Discipline and behavioral support: Practices, pitfalls, and promises. *Effective School Practices, 17,* 10–22.

Todd, A. W., Horner, R. H., Sugai, G., & Colvin, G. (1999). Individualizing school-wide discipline for students with chronic problem behaviors: A team approach. *Effective School Practices, 17,* 72–82.

Umbreit, J. (1995). Functional assessment and intervention in a regular classroom setting for the disruptive behavior of a student with Attention Deficit Hyperactivity Disorder. *Behavioral Disorders, 20,* 267–278.

U.S. Department of Education. (1999). *National educational goals report: Building a nation of learners.* Retrieved September 27, 2000 from the World Wide Web: http://www.negp.gov/reports/99rpt.pdf

Walker, H., Colvin, G., & Ramsey, E. (1995). *Antisocial behavior in public schools: Strategies and best practices.* Pacific Grove, CA: Brooks/Cole.

Wilcox, B. L., Turnbull, H. R. III, & Turnbull, A. (1999–2000/this issue). Behavioral issues and IDEA: Positive behavioral interventions and supports and the functional behavioral assessment in the disciplinary context. *Exceptionality, 8,* 173–187.

EXCEPTIONALITY, *8*(3), 173–187

Behavioral Issues and IDEA: Positive Behavioral Interventions and Supports and the Functional Behavioral Assessment in the Disciplinary Context

Brennan L. Wilcox, H. Rutherford Turnbull III, and Ann P. Turnbull

Beach Center on Families and Disability
University of Kansas

Positive behavioral interventions and supports (PBS) is the federal law's preferred strategy for dealing with challenging behavior by students with disabilities. The Individuals With Disabilities Education Act (IDEA) requires that PBS be considered in all cases of students whose behavior impedes their learning or the learning of others, reflecting IDEA's preference for use of state-of-the-art technology in special education. We believe that when schools take disciplinary actions against students with disabilities, PBS requirements will nearly always be at issue. This article describes the ramifications of IDEA's PBS requirements in the context of disciplinary situations, including the interplay of PBS issues with functional behavioral assessment and behavioral intervention plans.

Since its enactment, the Individuals With Disabilities Education Act (IDEA) has governed the rights of students with disabilities and the duties of schools to provide them a free, appropriate education (20 U.S.C. § 1400 *et seq.* (1999); 34 C.F.R. § 300.1 *et seq.* (1999)). It also has created roles for parents and school personnel to enter into a special partnership (A. Turnbull & Turnbull, 2001) for determining the students' needs and deciding how to fulfill those needs.

One area in which IDEA has had and will continue to have some impact is in school disciplinary matters. IDEA balances (a) the requirement that schools provide each child with

---

Requests for reprints should be sent to Brennan L. Wilcox, Beach Center on Families and Disability, University of Kansas, 3111 Haworth Hall, University of Kansas, Lawrence, KS 66045. E-mail: wilcox@dole.lsi.ukans.edu

an appropriate education in the least restrictive environment with (b) the need of schools to maintain an environment for all students that is both safe and conducive to learning.

For students with disabilities whose behavior is especially challenging (impedes their learning or the learning of others), IDEA strongly encourages the use of positive behavioral interventions and supports (PBS), a research-supported strategy for dealing with impeding behavior. This article generally explains the basic principles of IDEA and its disciplinary procedures. It focuses on explaining PBS, its role within IDEA, its relation to disciplinary situations, the relation of PBS to functional behavioral assessment (FBA) and behavioral intervention plan (BIP) requirements, and the roles and duties of general educators in these matters. The reader should bear in mind that this article involves analysis of federal law only. Individual states must incorporate federal rules as a minimum but may choose to adopt rules that are more restrictive.

IDEA AND ITS SIX PRINCIPLES

IDEA governs the education of children with disabilities through six major principles. These principles have been discussed at length by Turnbull and Turnbull (2000) but are discussed briefly here.

The first of the six principles is "zero reject." Zero reject is a rule against excluding any child with a disability from a free appropriate public education. It provides, among other things, that although the student might be disciplined, he or she might not be subjected to any cessation of educational services (20 U.S.C. §§ 1412 (a)(1), 1415 (k) (1999)). For example, even if a student is properly expelled from a school, the school district must continue to educate the student, although in another setting. Zero reject also provides that a student's public education will be at no cost to the parents (20 U.S.C. §§ 1412 (a)(1), 1401 (8) (1999)).

The second principle is "nondiscriminatory evaluation." This principle is a rule of fair evaluation of the student to determine whether the student has a disability and, if so, what special education and related services are required for the student (20 U.S.C. § 1414 (a)–(c) (1999)). To carry out a fair evaluation, the school must assess the student, interdisciplinarily, across a variety of domains (cognitive, behavioral, developmental, and physical) and in those specific areas in which the student might have (or is already known to have) a disability (20 U.S.C. § 1414 (b) (1999)). Among other things, this principle also provides that the student's parents are members of the team that evaluates the student (20 U.S.C. § 1414 (b)(4), (d)(1)(B)(i) (1999) and that they have the right to secure (sometimes at the cost of the school) and have the school consider any evaluations conducted by qualified individuals who are not employees or contractors of the school (20 U.S.C. §§ 1414 (c)(1), 1415 (b)(1) (1999); 34 C.F.R. § 300.502 (1999)).

The third principle is "appropriate education." This is a rule requiring individualization of special education (20 U.S.C. § 1401 (25) (1999); 34 C.F.R. § 300.26 (1999)) and related services (20 U.S.C. § 1401 (22) (1999); 34 C.F.R. § 300.24 (1999)). Just as the student's parents are members of the nondiscriminatory evaluation team (20 U.S.C. § 1414 (b)(4) (1999)), they also are members of the student's Individualized Education Program (IEP) team (20 U.S.C. § 1414 (d)(1)(B)(i) (1999); 34 C.F.R. §§ 300.344, 300.345 (1999)). This team is required to base the student's IEP and related services on the student's evaluation (20 U.S.C. § 1414 (d) (1999); 34 C.F.R. §§ 300.346, 300.347, 300.552 (1999)). The purpose of appropriate education is to assure specified outcomes for the student (20 U.S.C. § 1400 (c)(5)(E)(ii) (1999))—adult lives that are productive and independent to the maximum extent possible. The linchpin of an appropriate education is the student's IEP (20 U.S.C. § 1414 (d) (1999)), and the standards for determining whether a student has an appropriate education are that the school follows proper IDEA procedure and that the IEP offers an opportunity for the student to benefit from special education and any other services provided (*Board of Education v. Rowley*, 1982). An appropriate education includes, among other things, provisions regarding FBAs, BIPs, and PBS, as we explain more fully later.

The fourth of IDEA's principles is "least restrictive environment" (LRE). LRE is a rule of access to and progression through the general curriculum (defined as the academic, extracurricular, and other school activities that make up the same curriculum as that for students without disabilities; see 34 C.F.R. §§ 300.347, 300.553 (1999)). To have that access and opportunity to benefit, the student is entitled to receive supplementary aids and services as specified by the student's IEP team (of which, as noted earlier, the parents are members; 20 U.S.C. §§ 1401 (29), 1412 (a)(5) (1999)).

Significantly, Congress regards special education to be a service, not a place to which students are sent (20 U.S.C. § 1400 (c)(5)(C) (1999)). Accordingly, the legal presumption is that the student will be educated, to the maximum amount appropriate for the student, with students who do not have disabilities (20 U.S.C. § 1412 (a)(5) (1999)). This presumption may be set aside only if the "nature or severity of the disability is such that education in regular classes with the use of supplementary aids and services cannot be achieved satisfactorily" (34 C.F.R. § 300.550 (1999)). Even in such cases, however, the local educational agency (LEA) must provide a proper continuum of available services to ensure that the student is taught in the most inclusive setting possible (34 C.F.R. § 300.551 (1999)). The student's IEP team, supplemented by general educators and school administrators, determines the student's placement and is required to justify why access to the general curriculum should not be afforded, with supports (34 C.F.R. § 300.347 (1999)).

The fifth and sixth principles are, respectively, "procedural due process" (sometimes called procedural safeguards) and "parent–student participation." These rules create checks and balances. They are ways for assuring that the student benefits from being in school and that the school is providing the services and placements required by the other principles (see *Board of Education v. Rowley*, 1982; 34 C.F.R. §§ 300.500–300.589 (1999)). They also assure shared decision making concerning the student's education (20 U.S.C. § 1414 (d)(1)(B)(i) (1999); 34 C.F.R. §§ 300.344 (a)(1), 300.345 (1999)).

DEFINING POSITIVE BEHAVIORAL INTERVENTIONS, STRATEGIES, AND SUPPORTS

As described here, the implementation of PBS is both useful and necessary to ensure that schools meet IDEA's six principles. However, a teacher or other staff member might well ask, as do many other professionals and parents, "What is meant by positive behavioral interventions, strategies, and supports?" Without a definition, practitioners are apt to be lost: An undefined term is difficult (one might say impossible) to operationalize. IDEA uses the terms *positive behavioral interventions*, *strategies*, and *supports* (20 U.S.C. § 1414 (d)(3)(B)(i) (1999)), but this term is not defined by IDEA, its regulations, or the department's commentary on the regulations.

Within the research literature and practitioners' lexicon, the term is abbreviated and known as PBS and refers to a particular set of methods for dealing with "impeding behavior." PBS involves the "application of positive behavioral interventions and systems to achieve socially important behavior change" (Sugai et al., 1999, p. 6). PBS has four interrelated components: (a) systems change activities, (b) environmental alterations activities, (c) skill instruction activities, and (d) behavioral consequence activities (see H. R. Turnbull, Turnbull, Wilcox, Sailor, & Wickham, 1999). Together, these constitute a

> behaviorally-based systems approach [which is applied] to enhanc[e] the capacity of schools, families, and communities to design effective environments that improve the fit or link between research-validated practices and the environments in which teaching and learning occurs. Attention is focused on creating and sustaining school environments that improve lifestyle results (personal, health, social, family, work, recreation, etc.) for all children and youth by making problem behavior less effective, efficient, and relevant, and desired behavior more functional. In addition, the use of culturally appropriate interventions is emphasized .... At the core, PBS is the integration of behavioral science, practical interventions, social values, and a systems perspective. (Sugai et al., 1999, p. 7)

PBS can be and is being applied on a school-wide basis in many schools to improve behavior in the classroom more generally. Application on a school-wide basis aids in the IDEA-required facilitation of PBS for children with disabilities. For more information on practice-oriented issues regarding PBS, please see Sugai et al. (1999) and H. R. Turnbull et al. (1999).

APPLYING PBS UNDER IDEA

There are two situations under IDEA that implicate the use of PBS. The first relates to the student's IEP and "impeding" behavior. The second relates to discipline.

Impeding Behavior

For a student whose behavior impedes his or her learning or that of others, the IEP team, whether initially developing or later reviewing or revising the student's IEP, must "consider, when appropriate, strategies, including positive behavioral interventions, strategies, and supports to address that behavior" (20 U.S.C. § 1414 (d)(3)(B)(i) (1999); see also 34 C.F.R. §§ 300.346, 300.121 (1999); 64 Fed. Reg. 12,618–12,626 (1999)). This language allows the IEP team to consider other strategies but requires it to consider PBS.

The first inquiry is what is impeding behavior? Neither IDEA itself nor its regulations, nor departmental commentary on the regulations, define *impede*. In the absence of an "official" definition, we define impeding behaviors as those that

1. Impede the learning of the student or of others and include those behaviors that are externalizing (e.g., verbal abuse, aggression, self-injury, or property destruction); are internalizing (e.g., physical or social withdrawal, depression, passivity, resistance, social or physical isolation, or noncompliance); are manifestations of biological or neurological conditions (e.g., obsessions, compulsions, stereotypes, or irresistible impulses); are manifestations of abuse, neglect, exploitation, or maltreatment; or are disruptive (e.g., annoying, confrontational, defiant, or taunting).
2. Could cause the student to be disciplined pursuant to any state or federal law or regulations, or could cause any consideration of a change of the student's educational placement.
3. Are recurring consistently and therefore require FBA and the systematic and frequent application of PBS (H. R. Turnbull et al., 1999).

Our definition has several benefits. First, it includes all behaviors; it is pragmatic and not limiting. Second, it comes into play in cases of both impeding behavior and discipline. Third, it requires more than one event or episode (although practitioners are free, in their professional judgment, to develop PBS for a student who has a single event or episode of impeding behavior). Fourth, it fills the void that the department has created by failing to define *impede,* and it thereby guides practitioners, due process hearing officers, and judges who must interpret IDEA.

By requiring LEAs to consider PBS when "impede" is an issue, IDEA puts teeth into Congress's finding that students have not benefitted from "replicable research." Even in its most recent amendments to IDEA (1997), Congress stated that implementation of the law had been impeded by an "insufficient focus on applying replicable research on proven methods of teaching and learning for children with disabilities" (20 U.S.C. § 1400 (c)(4) (1999)). This statement has significance in that Congress mentions only PBS (a proven method backed by replicable research) as its preferred means for dealing with impeding behavior. This supports our upcoming contention that IDEA has created a rebuttable presumption that PBS should be used in these cases. Moreover, IDEA sets the stage for using PBS in the event of student discipline. Let us explain why we reach these conclusions.

PBS in Disciplinary Situations

First, let us acknowledge that IDEA does not expressly require an LEA to consider PBS when disciplining a student. It seems to us, however, that disciplinary situations might require a LEA to develop an IEP for a student who does not already have one; this is so because discipline might trigger the student's referral to, and then inclusion in, special education and because every student in special education who is protected by IDEA must have an IEP (20 U.S.C. § 1414 (d) (1999)). If an IEP is being developed because of the student's impeding behavior, the IEP team must consider using PBS. Moreover, discipline also might trigger a review or revision of an existing IEP, or both, in which case the "consider" requirements also apply (20 U.S.C. § 1414 (d)(3), (d)(4) (1999)). It seems then that, on the basis of the statute's own language, discipline triggers FBA, BIP, and PBS requirements.

There is a very practical implication of that interpretation—namely, that any behavior that triggers discipline should be modified and that PBS is an effective (and preferred) intervention to change behavior. Indeed, although it might be too late to use PBS as a prevention strategy, because the student's behavior already has resulted in discipline, it is not too late to use PBS as a strategy to prevent further occurrences of behavior that cause the child to be subject to discipline. An argument is that, although one incident triggering discipline has occurred, others can be prevented by the use of PBS.

Second, we believe a fair reading of the discipline provisions justifies the conclusion that PBS at the very least should be, and at the optimum must be, an outcome of the disciplinary process. Let us show why we reach that result by analyzing IDEA's discipline provisions.

IDEA disciplinary procedure. As previously mentioned, IDEA attempts to balance two concerns: (a) the requirement that children with disabilities receive an appropriate education in the least restrictive environment and (b) the maintenance of a safe environment for all students that is conducive to learning. The balancing of these two concerns obviously is not always easy. Moreover, the issue of school safety and discipline has caused a great deal of concern for schools and parents of children with disabilities throughout the nation. Indeed, some people mistakenly believe that IDEA does not allow children with disabilities to be removed from the classroom, regardless of any danger they might pose to themselves or others. As discussed next, however, IDEA does provide means to ensure that schools are able to balance these two concerns.

First, it is necessary to understand why IDEA protects the educational needs of children with disabilities who have behavioral challenges. IDEA's appropriate education guarantees historically arise from a civil rights context. In the opening section of IDEA, Congress recites how children with disabilities historically have been denied an appropriate education and have been excluded improperly and systematically from being educated with their peers (20 U.S.C. § 1400 (c) (1999)). Congress concluded that, as a result, these children were denied equal educational opportunity. This history of unequal treatment is the basis for IDEA's requirements that an appropriate education be provided to every child (even those who are removed from the regular classroom altogether). Congress was careful, however, to preserve schools' power to ensure the safety of the school environment. Although school personnel must follow certain procedures when removing a child with a disability from the classroom, IDEA does grant them the authority necessary to maintain the safety of all children if one child's behavior poses a substantial threat to that safety.

It is helpful to notice that there are at least three separate but closely connected discipline provisions. The first gives an LEA the authority to move a student from his or her current placement to another of the LEA's choosing (including temporary suspension) for up to 10 consecutive schooldays for any violation of the school's code of conduct, or to an appropriate interim alternative educational setting for up to 45 days if the child carries or possesses a weapon or illegal drugs on school premises (20 U.S.C. § 1415 (k)(1)(A) (1999); 34 C.F.R. § 300.520 (1999)). In addition, if keeping the student in his or her current placement would be "substantially likely to result in injury" to the student or others, the LEA may remove the student from that placement if a judge or hearing officer determines that the child should be placed in an interim alternative educational setting (20 U.S.C. § 1415 (k)(2) (1999); 34 C.F.R. § 300.521 (1999)). In both cases, the LEA must act in a nondiscriminatory manner (i.e., discipline the child in the same way it disciplines children without disabilities), and the LEA must continue to provide free appropriate public education services after 10 cumulative days of removal within the same school year (20 U.S.C. § 1412 (a)(1) (1999); 34 C.F.R. §§ 300.520, 300.121 (d) (1999)).

The second provision limits an LEA's authority to remove students through the "manifestation rule." Under this provision, an LEA may not discipline the student by changing his or her placement (the regulations define "change of placement") if the behavior for which the student is disciplined is a "manifestation" of the student's disability (20 U.S.C. § 1415 (k) (1999); 34 C.F.R. §§ 300.519, 300.523, 300.524 (1999)). The agency may, however, review and change the IEP as necessary to address the behavior (and must do so if the IEP or services currently provided are inadequate; 34 C.F.R. § 300.523 (f) (1999)). Note that there is an exception to this rule where the child's parents agree to the change of placement.

Finally, IDEA provides for a means to address the behavior:

> If the local education agency did not conduct a functional behavioral assessment and implement a behavioral intervention plan for such child before the behavior that resulted [in the discipline], the agency shall convene an IEP meeting to develop an assessment plan to address that behavior. (20 U.S.C. § 1415 (k)(1)(B), 1999; see also 34 C.F.R. § 300.520 (b)(1)(i) (1999))

"As soon as practicable" after completion of the assessments (FBA) required by that plan, the IEP team must meet again to "develop appropriate behavioral interventions to address that behavior and shall implement those interventions" (34 C.F.R. § 300.520 (b)(2) (1999)). The FBA and BIP are required when "either first removing the child for more than 10 school days in a school year or commencing a removal that constitutes a change of placement ... [including changes of placement for weapon or drug violations...]" (34 C.F.R. § 300.520 (b)(1) (1999)).

Now that we know what an LEA may do (its authority), its limitations (manifestation determination), and what benefit accrues to the student (FBA and BIP), let us consider the relation of these provisions to PBS.

Granted, the FBA and BIP requirements do not mention PBS in connection with discipline. When, however, the need for discipline arises, the IEP team (as noted previously) is required to develop, review, or revise any BIP for the sole purpose of addressing the behavior for which the student was disciplined (20 U.S.C. § 1415 (k)(1)(B) (1999); 34 C.F.R. § 300.520 (b)(1), (b)(2) (1999)). If it has to develop the plan in the first place, it must do so by conducting an FBA before implementing a plan based on the assessment (20 U.S.C. § 1415 (k)(1)(B) (1999); 34 C.F.R. § 300.520 (b)(1), (b)(2) (1999)). We believe it is logical to conclude that because the FBA and BIP are created by the IEP team and should be included in the IEP, their development or review constitute a review of the IEP, triggering the "consider" requirements (34 C.F.R. § 300.346 (b) (1999)).

Moreover, FBA is inseparable in the research and practice literature from PBS (Sugai et al., 1999; H. R. Turnbull et al., 1999). Accordingly, we believe that the IEP team at least must consider PBS to address behavior for which a student is disciplined. In addition, the department has explained in its commentary on the controlling regulation (34 C.F.R. § 300.520 (1999)) that PBS, if contained in the IEP, themselves might compose the BIP:

> If, under § 300.346 (a) and (c), IEP teams are proactively addressing a child's behavior that impedes the child's learning or that of others in the development of IEPs, those strategies, including positive behavioral interventions, strategies and supports in the child's IEP will constitute the behavioral intervention plan that the IEP team reviews under paragraph (b)(2) of [§ 300.520]. (64 Fed. Reg. 12,620 (1999))

In addition, the Department's commentary on IDEA regulations states that "school officials have powerful incentives to implement positive behavioral interventions, strategies and supports whenever behavior interferes with the important teaching and learning activities of school" (64 Fed. Reg. 12,588 (1999)).

It therefore seems to us that, whenever the IEP team is required to examine an existing BIP (pursuant to 34 C.F.R. § 300.520 (1999)), the team necessarily will reexamine the extent to which an FBA and possibly a positive BIP should be undertaken and developed. The IEP team thus could save time and extra steps by conducting an FBA and developing a PBS plan during creation of the IEP. Those extra steps saved are conducting an FBA and developing a BIP at the time of the discipline (64 Fed. Reg. 12,620 (1999)).

PBS AS A PREFERRED INTERVENTION AND A REBUTTABLE PRESUMPTION

It is one thing to analyze IDEA to guide practitioners. It is altogether another to explain the essential nature of IDEA. To do that, let us bear in mind that law is a form of social engineering: It shapes people's behavior.

Among the ways the law does so is by creating presumptions in favor of certain procedures and outcomes and by linking procedures to outcomes. The most familiar presumption is found in the criminal law: A person is presumed innocent until found guilty. Another is found in IDEA: A student with a disability is to be educated with students who do not have disabilities unless that placement would not benefit that student or would harm other students (20 U.S.C. § 1412 (a)(5) (1999); 34 C.F.R. §§ 300.550–300.556 (1999)). These are rebuttable presumptions: When the evidence shows that a defendant is guilty, the presumption of innocence is overturned, and when there is no benefit from inclusive education, then separate education is warranted.

Now, let us see how IDEA engages in social engineering by using presumptions. We believe that IDEA has created a rebuttable presumption in favor of the use of PBS. This is so because IDEA mentions only PBS as an intervention strategy that the IEP team must consider in the case of impeding behavior. True, the team might consider other interventions, but it must consider PBS. We believe that a fair conclusion from the clear language of IDEA is that, if the IEP team considers other interventions, it may do so only in comparison to PBS and must have adequate cause for adopting another intervention over PBS when both are appropriate. Why else would IDEA require the team to consider PBS if it did not also want the team to use PBS?

In our opinion, a presumption in favor of PBS is also a presumption against the use of aversive interventions. PBS rewards desirable behavior, making it functional, and removes rewards from undesirable behavior, making it less functional. Aversive interventions, on the other hand, do not reward desirable behavior but attempt instead to punish undesirable behavior until it is extinguished (Sugai et al., 1999; H. R. Turnbull et al., 1999). In our view, these two approaches are antithetical, and, thus, preference for one is preference against the other.

Undoubtedly, IDEA does not prohibit aversive interventions explicitly, but commentary by the Department of Education supports our conclusion that there is a rebuttable presumption in favor of PBS and against aversive interventions:

> Regarding what behavioral interventions and strategies can be used, and whether the use of aversive behavioral management strategies is prohibited under these regulations, the needs of the individual child are of paramount importance in determining the behavioral management strategies that are appropriate for inclusion in the child's IEP. In making these determinations, the primary focus must be on ensuring that the behavioral management strategies in the child's IEP reflect the Act's requirement for the use of positive behavioral interventions and strategies. (65 Fed. Reg. 12,589 (1999))

It seems to us that the quoted language—"the act's requirement"—and the context of this paragraph of commentary strongly reinforce the conclusion that we have reached—namely, that the IDEA provisions related to PBS create at least a rebuttable presumption against the use of aversive interventions and in favor of the use of positive interventions.

Aversive interventions generally involve the delivery of pain, result in tissue damage, or rely on humiliation as a planned consequence (H. R. Turnbull et al., 1999). We define *aversive interventions* to include the following, without limitation:

1. Corporal punishment, including head butting, spanking, slapping, paddling, water spraying, sensory deprivation, maintenance in any physically painful position, or any other intervention that is designed or likely to cause physical pain.
2. Rooms, boxes, or other structures or spaces from which the student cannot exit readily, and the use of seclusionary or isolation time out.
3. Noxious substances, toxic or otherwise unpleasant sprays (including water sprays), mists, or substances released in proximity to the student's face or any especially sensitive part of the student's body.
4. Deprivation of health-sustaining necessities, including meals, water, other nourishment, fresh air, sleep, shelter, bedding, physical comfort, access to toilet facilities, or prescribed medication.
5. Serial suspensions that constitute a change of placement as defined by IDEA (20 U.S.C. § 1415 (k) (1999); 34 C.F.R. § 300.519 (b) (1999)).

6. Treatment of a demeaning nature, including interventions that are designed or likely to subject the student to verbal abuse, ridicule, or humiliation or are likely to cause emotional trauma for that student or adverse behavioral reactions from others.
7. Electric shock.
8. Any interventions or methods that temporarily or otherwise deprive the student of the use of one or more of his or her senses.
9. Any interventions or methods that produce or are likely to produce tissue damage.
10. The unwarranted use of drugs or other medical interventions, where "unwarranted" means not justified by, and prescribed by a physician for, any reasonable medical purpose related to the student.
11. Any interventions or methods that preclude adequate supervision of the student.
12. Any interventions or methods, not authorized by the agency's policies, that are inconsistent with these criteria. (H. R. Turnbull et al., 1999)

Accordingly, no state or local educational agency should, in our opinion, use any such interventions, techniques, or strategies on any student or incorporate any of them into any student's IEP or into any student's BIP (which, as we have explained, should be part of the student's IEP and reflect PBS as an intervention). Neither (in our judgment) should a student's BIP include the use of physical or mechanical restraint devices or techniques except in the cases where they are required to prevent self-injury or promote normal body positioning or physical functioning (as prescribed by trained personnel and accompanied by PBS; H. R. Turnbull et al., 1999). In cases of emergency—for example, where the student's behavior poses a clear and present danger of serious physical harm to the student or to others and PBS strategies have not been developed or are ineffective—restraint might be legally justifiable. However, because the goal is to minimize the use of that technique, emergency interventions should be used only long enough to eliminate the clear and present danger and never as a regular substitute for PBS interventions (see H. R. Turnbull et al., 1999). Moreover, a full range of PBS should be available and used to ensure adequate less restrictive alternatives to restraint.

BOARD OF EDUCATION V. ROWLEY, THE DEFINITION OF APPROPRIATE EDUCATION, AND PBS

Thus far, we have defined PBS and *impede*, analyzed IDEA and reached the conclusion that local educational agencies and practitioners should use PBS in situations involving impeding behavior and discipline, explained that PBS is the presumptively correct intervention, and argued for limitations on aversives and restraints. There is more, however, to favor PBS in impede and discipline situations. That "more" is the requirement that local educational agencies provide an "appropriate" education to students with disabilities, a requirement best understood in light of the first special education case to reach the United States Supreme Court.

When, in 1982, the Court decided *Board of Education v. Rowley*, its decision created two key tests for determining whether a student has received an appropriate education. These are known as the process test and the benefit test.

The process test of *Board of Education v. Rowley* (1982) essentially requires that local educational agencies must follow IDEA's procedural requirements to provide an appropriate education. If proper IDEA procedures are not followed, then in most cases a court will hold that the student has not received an appropriate education (H. Turnbull & Turnbull, 2000).

The benefit test of *Board of Education v. Rowley* (1982) requires that the student receive benefit from the services provided. Even if the proper procedures are followed, a student is not receiving an appropriate education if he or she is not receiving a benefit from the services provided. This need not be the maximum benefit, but services provided must result in some substantive level of benefit. No "bright-line" rule has been established to determine the exact level of benefit required, but courts have held that the benefit must be more than de minimis and that the student must not be regressing (H. Turnbull & Turnbull, 2000).

Meeting the Process Test for PBS

As noted, a student's IEP team is required to consider the use of PBS for a student who exhibits impeding behavior. Therefore, procedural requirements regarding PBS revolve around the issue of what it means to properly consider PBS. Bear in mind that PBS relies on the proper use of FBA.

Defining consider*: The process of consideration.* In our judgment, the word *consider* requires the IEP team to (a) understand what PBS is and how it works, (b) have the ability to implement PBS, (c) engage in a discussion of whether to employ PBS, and (d) set out the reasoning behind their decision whether to employ PBS.

Here is why we offer that advice to local educational agencies and practitioners: The IEP team members truly cannot consider what they do not understand, and it is meaningless for them to consider a futile option, one they cannot implement, even rudimentarily. Furthermore, for them to consider any intervention, they must weigh the benefits and drawbacks of PBS and give one or more rationale for their decision. A result without a reason is not persuasive or defensible; it can be attacked as not professionally sound.

The team is not required to use PBS, only to consider whether to use PBS. Thus, we conclude that the IEP team may consider the use of other strategies than, or in addition to, PBS or to use no interventions at all. Nothing in IDEA prevents a team from considering such interventions as a therapeutic drug regimen (relying on medical advice); the use of nonpositive interventions (which are difficult to justify under the rebuttable presumption given to PBS); or the continuation, modification, or discontinuation of present (positive or other) interventions (if any).

The importance of proper documentation. It seems to us advisable for the team to document its decision-making process by minutes that reflect that it followed these "consider" criteria. Because IDEA creates a rebuttable presumption in favor of PBS, someone—a team member, such as a parent, who is unhappy with a team recommendation to not use PBS—might challenge the team's decision-making process and the results of that process. That person might ask, Why was it not appropriate to consider PBS? What other strategies were considered? What factors ruled out PBS? If an attack is made on the process for the team's decision making, then documentation of the process can be evidence that the team met its legal duty to consider PBS.

As we pointed out, the IEP team must consider PBS for a student with impeding behavior as it develops, reviews, or revises the student's IEP (34 C.F.R. § 300.346 (a), (b) (1999)). There is, however, more to the team's duties. If the team determines that the child is in need of "a particular device or service (including an intervention, accommodation, or other program modification) in order for the child to receive [a free appropriate public education], the IEP team must include a statement to that effect in the child's IEP" (34 C.F.R. § 300.346 (c) (1999)). Thus, if the IEP team determines that a student requires PBS of any type or degree, the team must include a statement to that effect in the student's IEP.

Moreover, it seems to us that the team should not develop a PBS plan unless the LEA first has conducted an FBA (Sugai et al., 1999; H. R. Turnbull et al., 1999). Consistent with good practice, the FBA should be conducted across all settings in which the student lives, and a written report of the FBA process and results should be prepared and entered into the student's file and attached to his or her IEP (Sugai et al., 1999; H. R. Turnbull et al., 1999).

Some school personnel might think that some plans might be too complex to be part of a student's IEP, because the plans might require a large number of minor changes to be made frequently and because having an IEP meeting to approve every change is administratively burdensome. However, if the changes do not affect the plan's core purpose and methods, we believe it is defensible to make them without an IEP meeting, especially if the IEP itself allows such changes. For example, the plan could include schedules for altering specified interventions or supports or the frequency or duration thereof without necessity for reconvening the IEP team (see H. R. Turnbull et al., 1999). The school psychologist (or other team member with similar qualifying expertise) should be careful to identify which changes are core and which are not and to assure that the IEP gives the team the necessary—but not too much—flexibility.

Meeting the Benefit Test for PBS

As we have noted, the team must consider PBS and may consider other interventions to address the student's behavior (34 C.F.R. § 300.346 (a)(2)(i) (1999)). In our opinion, address means that the interventions must be targeted at preventing, reducing, replacing, or otherwise appropriately dealing with the behavior (or behaviors). We rest our conclusion on the benefit standard in *Board of Education v. Rowley* (1982). There, the Court interpreted IDEA's requirement of an appropriate education to mean that the student must be provided services that will enable the student to benefit from special education. In the PBS–consider context, the benefit standard requires that any strategy to address a student's behavior must benefit by changing the student's behavior and thereby strengthening the student's ability to benefit from special education.

We believe that this benefit is required only when the student is the designated beneficiary of PBS—that is, only when the student's IEP calls for PBS or an FBA and BIP. For example, a student who requires other special education or related services (but not individualized PBS) but receives PBS services as part of a school-wide program (it seems to us) will not be denied an appropriate education solely because the school-wide PBS services failed to provide a benefit for the child. However, for the student who requires individualized behavioral planning under IDEA, PBS, and behavioral planning must provide a benefit.

However, use of PBS with any and all students (school-wide), and attempting to provide a benefit therefrom, is in our judgment best practice, regardless of requirement by law. Similarly, providing a higher level of benefit than that required by law is also best practice. These best practices benefit individual students and also provide school-wide benefits, including environments that are more conducive to learning (i.e., fewer class disruptions; Sugai et al., 1999).

Here a note about the use of PBS in a school-wide context is warranted. If the school has adopted PBS on a school-wide scale, the job of the general education teacher who must implement PBS for one child with a disability becomes radically easier. Where school-wide implementation occurs, the teacher will be faced only with changing the degree of intervention and support for any particular child and need not implement PBS as a wholly different form of intervening with children whose behaviors impede their own learning as well as the learning of others.

At a time when school safety is a national concern (20 U.S.C. § 1415 (k) (1999)), when outcome-driven education is the norm (20 U.S.C. § 1414 (d)(1)(A)(i) and (v) (1999)), when students with disabilities are expected to participate in and progress through the general curriculum (20 U.S.C. § 1414 (d)(1)(A)(iii) (1999)), and when the application of research-based technology is expected at the state and local level (20 U.S.C. § 1400 (c)(4) (1999)), we think that PBS is a nearly ideal intervention. It can come into play in matters of discipline, must be considered when behaviors impede learning outcomes, must be applied across all educational settings, is a technique with which general educators must at least be acquainted, and is indeed a research-based strategy.

The impediments to the use of PBS are, however, not insignificant. As a strategy, it is still unfamiliar to many educators and school staff and to many faculty in institutions of higher education where general and special educators are trained. Moreover, it can be a time- and labor-intensive strategy for some students. When it is required, some school staff might want to minimize its scope (and thus its benefits), adopting a "once over lightly" that might be legally sufficient but not programmatically effective.

What teachers and other staff should bear in mind is that IDEA sets minimum standards for good practice. Our position is that the diligent and informed application of PBS to circumstances of impeded learning and discipline is the best assurance, now and in the future, that schools will be said to have carried out their mission: to provide an appropriate education for children with disabilities. Here, then, is a strategy that benefits schools, staff, and children with disabilities. IDEA sets the legal framework for the strategy, but school staff have the opportunity—we argue the duty—to fulfill the law's promise of an effective education.

ROLES OF THE GENERAL EDUCATOR

Because IDEA promotes inclusion of children with disabilities to the greatest extent possible in the general educational classroom, it is natural that the role of the general educator is extremely important to the success of that goal. It is important that general educators understand the special challenges that these students face and are trained to provide the support that these children require to succeed. Further, these educators need to be supported in this same regard to ensure that they can balance their duties with respect to children with special needs and their duties to the classroom as a whole. Thus, we note here the special roles played by general educators in regard to PBS and IDEA.

The General Educator as Member of the IEP Team

Each child's IEP team must include at least one of the child's general education teachers (20 U.S.C. § 1414 (d)(1)(B)(ii) (1999); 34 C.F.R. § 300.344 (a)(2) (1999)). Membership on the IEP team can entail involvement in a number of different meetings and activities, including evaluation and reevaluation of the child's disability and functioning and IEP planning and implementation (including FBA and BIP development and implementation).

It is important to note that the general education teacher need not participate in each and every IEP team meeting. However, the involvement of general education teachers in certain IEP team decisions is strongly emphasized by IDEA. IDEA states that the "regular" (general) education teacher

> must, to the extent appropriate, participate in the development, review, and revision of the child's IEP, including assisting in the determination of (1) appropriate positive behavioral interventions and strategies for the child; and (2) supplementary aids and services, program modifications or supports for school personnel that will be provided for the child, consistent with 300.347 (a)(3). (34 C.F.R. § 300.346 (d) (1999))

Role of the General Educator in PBS Implementation

To reiterate from the previous quote, the role of the general education teacher as a member of the IEP team includes assisting in the determination of "appropriate positive behavioral interventions and strategies for the child [and] supplementary aids and services, program modifications or supports for school personnel that will be provided for the child ...." The general education teacher is very important to the success of PBS. Proper implementation of PBS involves rather extensive record keeping to assess the functionality of the child's behavior (FBA). This will include behavioral record keeping in all environments, including that of the general education classroom. Further, once FBA has occurred and PBS are agreed on, it is up to the general education teacher to implement these interventions and supports within their classroom.

CONCLUSIONS

This article has explained the basic principles of IDEA and its disciplinary procedure. Through an explanation of PBS, it is obvious that FBA and BIP are a vital part of IDEA disciplinary procedure. This also has shown the relation of PBS to these procedures and its importance in implementing IDEA and meeting its six principles.

ACKNOWLEDGMENTS

This article was supported in part by U.S. Department of Education Grant No. H326S980003. The opinions expressed herein do not necessarily reflect the position or policy of the Department, and no official endorsement by the Department should be inferred.

REFERENCES

Board of Education v. Rowley, 458 U.S. 176 (1982).

Individuals With Disabilities Education Act, 20 U.S.C. § 1400 *et seq.* (1999); 34 C.F.R. § 300.1 *et seq.* (1999); 64 Fed. Reg. 12,406–12,672 (1999).

Sugai, G., Horner, R., Dunlap, G., Lewis, T., Nelson, M., Scott, T., Liakupsin, C., Ruef, M., Sailor, W., Turnbull, A., Turnbull, H., Wickham, D., & Wilcox, B. (1999). *Applying positive behavioral support and functional behavioral assessment in schools.* Eugene, OR: Center on Behavioral Interventions and Supports, University of Oregon.

Turnbull, A., & Turnbull, H. (2001). *Families, professionals, and exceptionality: Collaborating for empowerment* (4th ed.). Upper Saddle River, NJ: Merrill/Prentice Hall.

Turnbull, H. R., Turnbull, A. P., Wilcox, B. L., Sailor, W., & Wickham, D. (1999). *Positive behavioral interventions and supports under the Individuals With Disabilities Education Act.* Lawrence, KS: Beach Center on Families and Disability, The University of Kansas.

Turnbull, H., & Turnbull, A. (with Wilcox, B., & Stowe, M.). (2000). *Free appropriate public education: The law and children with disabilities* (6th ed.). Denver, CO: Love.

EXCEPTIONALITY, *8*(3), 189–204

Functional Assessment and Comprehensive Early Intervention

Joshua K. Harrower, Lise Fox, Glen Dunlap, and Don Kincaid
Child and Family Studies
University of South Florida

Functional assessment has been shown to be an essential tool in developing effective behavior support plans for young children with challenging behavior. Such plans have been effective not only in reducing problem behavior and improving socially appropriate behavior, but also in preventing the development of further, more severe, problem behavior. The purpose of this article is to outline a process for conducting comprehensive early intervention based on a comprehensive assessment process that includes functional assessment. A case example is presented to further illustrate this process. Additional elements essential to the process, including family involvement, collaborative teaming, and implementing intervention in multiple environments, are discussed.

Functional assessment is an invaluable process for developing effective behavioral supports for people of all ages. For young children, a number of demonstrations have shown that functional assessment can result in interventions that reduce or eliminate serious problem behaviors while enhancing developmental trajectories and facilitating the acquisition of needed competencies (e.g., Dunlap & Fox, 1999a; Moes & Frea, 2000). In addition, a number of authors (e.g., Dunlap & Fox, 1996; Dunlap, Johnson, & Robbins, 1990; Reeve & Carr, in press) have advanced the argument that functional assessment and comprehensive assessment-based interventions have the potential to curtail the likelihood that the later lives of young children will be impaired by serious problem behaviors. In our view, the extent to which the assessment–intervention process will produce such widespread and durable effects is dependent on a number of considerations: the extent to which the process involves and centers around the child's family; the extent to which the assessment process incorporates a broad, lifestyle perspective and includes person-cen-

Requests for reprints should be sent to Joshua K. Harrower, University of South Florida, DARES–CFS–FMHI, University of South Florida, MHC 2113A, 13301 Bruce B. Downs Boulevard, Tampa, FL 33612. E-mail: harrower@fmhi.usf.edu

tered (and family-centered) planning; and the extent to which a comprehensive orientation to behavior support is adopted.

The remainder of this article provides brief discussions of important considerations and elements in the functional assessment and behavioral support processes, particularly as they relate to family-centered interventions with young children. Some of the issues and components are illustrated in a case study section, which provides the experience of a child and family who participated in a model of early intervention that we have been working on for the past several years (Fox, Dunlap, & Philbrick, 1997). The model is geared for children who have problem behaviors and extensive developmental challenges, such as autism. Indeed, much of this article's content is based on work conducted with children and families affected by pervasive disabilities; however, we emphasize that the considerations raised in the following discussion are likely to have widespread generality and applicability for all children whose lives are compromised by the presence of serious problem behaviors.

FUNCTIONAL ASSESSMENT AND FAMILY INVOLVEMENT

The process of functional assessment and positive behavior support in early intervention is based on a long line of research and practice (Dunlap et al., 1990; Dunlap & Fox, 1996, 1999a; Fox, Dunlap, & Buschbacher, in press; R. L. Koegel, Koegel, & Surratt, 1992; McEvoy et al., 1988). A crucial consideration when utilizing functional assessment in early intervention is that the entire rationale for conducting a functional assessment is to develop an effective assessment-based plan of intervention. Functional assessment is central to the approach for addressing problem behavior known as positive behavior support, which is referred to in the Individuals With Disabilities Education Act (IDEA, 1997) as "positive behavior interventions and supports" (Sugai et al., in press; Tilly et al., 1998). Positive behavior support refers to the application of effective, individualized approaches, based on a collaborative, assessment-based process, to develop appropriate behaviors and reduce problem behaviors in a manner that produces durable improvements in a person's lifestyle (L. K. Koegel, Koegel, & Dunlap, 1996; Rehabilitation Research & Training Center on Positive Behavioral Support, 2000).

Proponents of positive behavioral support advocate for a team-based approach (e.g., Bambara & Knoster, 1998; Hieneman & Dunlap, 1999) that includes input and participation from all individuals who are invested and involved in the life of the focus individual. Naturally, a team-based approach to a comprehensive functional assessment and positive behavioral support mandates a large measure of family involvement.

A COMPREHENSIVE FUNCTIONAL ASSESSMENT PROCESS

We believe that for family-centered early intervention to be fully comprehensive, it should incorporate not only the use of traditional functional assessment procedures, but also the use of person or family-centered planning processes. Although there is not, nor should there be, a specific format for this process, there are common features to be included in its implementation. A child's team must determine the specific strategies and account for the specific needs of the child, family, and team.

Person and Family-Centered Planning

Person-centered planning processes were designed to provide a mechanism for understanding individuals with developmental disabilities and to work with them and their supporters in achieving new experiences (O'Brien, O'Brien, & Mount, 1997). It is a creative process that emphasizes the identification of the strengths and capacities of the individual while using collaborative problem solving to seek solutions to barriers and difficulties. The goal of person-centered planning is the development of a circle of support that assists the individual in identifying and achieving a vision for the future (Forest & Lusthaus, 1987; Mount & Zwernick, 1988). Although these processes were developed and have been described primarily for adults and for facilitating transitional arrangements, they are also quite pertinent for young children and their families.

In the functional assessment and positive behavior support process, person-centered planning provides a vehicle for thinking creatively and bringing together a circle of support for the child with problem behavior. The person-centered planning process encourages the participation of family, friends, and professionals in contributing to a collective vision for supporting the child. It is an informal and intimate process where strategies and solutions are generated by reaching a holistic understanding of the child and family. This understanding guides and enhances the behavior support process by clarifying the goals and needs of the child and family while strengthening the shared commitment of support by the child's family, friends, and service providers.

Person-centered planning can inform the functional assessment process by providing information on the child's preferences, activities, and environments. As a result, person-centered planning lays a strong foundation for the development of an effective support plan. Person-centered planning might identify and address many of the global or broad ecological issues impacting the family and child's life. This information compliments the specific and precise information identified in traditional behavior assessment approaches. The resulting comprehensive assessment process brings the team to an understanding of the purpose and variables surrounding the child's behavior, as well as the family and team goals for the child. This increases the likelihood of developing a plan that will effectively support the family system, the child's use of appropriate behavior and access to an improved lifestyle, and the ongoing functioning of the team.

Functional Assessment

Functional assessment is defined as a process for developing an understanding of the interactions between a specified behavior and events in the environment (Horner & Carr, 1997). In particular, a functional assessment identifies the consequences that represent the behavior's function, or purpose, and the contextual events and circumstances that are predictable antecedents of the behavior (Foster-Johnson & Dunlap, 1993; O'Neill, Vaughn, & Dunlap, 1998; Tilly et al., 1998). By now, many articles and books have described useful direct and indirect methods for conducting functional assessments (e.g., O'Neill et al., 1997), and a substantial corpus of empirical research provides testimony to the efficacy and feasibility of the functional assessment approach (Carr et al., 1999; Repp & Horner, 1999).

Gathering information. There are two strategies for gathering information when conducting a functional assessment. The first is to talk to the family and other care providers who have direct knowledge of the child and the problem behavior. Families become partners in the functional assessment process by identifying the environments and activities where the child is most likely to have problem behavior and assisting the professional in conducting and interpreting observations (Albin, Lucyshyn, Horner, & Flannery, 1996). Parents are often so aware of the antecedents to severe problem behavior that they frequently engineer various preventative measures within the course of their daily activities. This is not surprising, as it serves the family well to avoid or prevent severe disruptions. Yet, if this kind of information is not effectively solicited from the family, a resulting plan that does not account for this information is likely to fail. For example, a family might change their dinner routine significantly and allow the toddler with problem behavior to snack all day because sitting in the high chair evokes a tantrum. In this case, it is important to know what accommodations are being made and how they might influence the development of desired behaviors (e.g., the ability to sit in a chair). Structured interviews offer a format for systematically collecting information about the nature of the problem behavior and can easily be tailored to address issues specific to early intervention. For example, information can be gathered regarding the child's activity patterns, play interactions, and symbolic development, all of which are relevant to the functional assessment of a young child's behavior.

The second strategy for information gathering in the functional assessment process is to observe the child within the settings and activities where problem behavior is likely to occur. Observations are conducted to validate or supplement the information gained from the functional assessment interview. Observations should provide information on the nature and intensity of problem behavior, antecedents or predictors of the problem behavior, the ways in which others respond to problem behavior, and the perceived functions of the problem behavior. This information might be collected using anecdotal recording, incident reports or crisis logs, time sampling techniques, and antecedent–behavior–consequence analysis (Horner, O'Neill, & Flannery, 1993; O'Neill et al., 1997; O'Neill et al., 1998). In addition, many of these methods have been found to be accurate in determining the functions of problem behavior displayed even by infant children (Weigle, 2000).

All too often, interventionists take a narrow approach to functional assessment that adheres to a limited contingency management model of consequences and immediate antecedents. This approach, however, is rarely adequate when dealing with severe problem behavior. For example, it is often the case that problem behaviors are evoked or exacerbated by internal discomfort or illness, and by general unhappiness with the social, curricular, or structural elements of a setting. To achieve durable, meaningful behavior change, it is often important for the functional assessment process to examine explicitly the possibility of such setting influences, and for intervention to include pertinent adjustments to such variables as medical treatment and daily routines (e.g., Dadson & Horner, 1993; Kennedy & Itkonen, 1993; Turnbull & Turnbull, 1996). Families are in a unique position to collect this type of information. For example, the child might appear to have more problem behavior following nights when the child has had little sleep. The family also might suspect that days that have a high pollen count and the child is bothered by allergies coincide with more problem behavior from their child. The professional can develop a simple observation checklist for the family to collect information of wakefulness, high pollen count as reported by the newspaper, and the level of problem behavior their child exhibits. After 1 or 2 weeks of data, patterns might be revealed that support or dispute the relation of problem behavior to those events.

As the support provider begins the process of functional assessment, it is critical that information is shared with the family about the purpose of the process and how information will be used in the development of a behavior support plan. Families are more likely to reveal information to providers when there is rapport and a trusting relationship (Fox, Vaughn, Dunlap, & Bucy, 1997). The value of a trusting relationship should not be underestimated. Family members have reported that they often feel judged when their children have problem behavior and might be reluctant to share information that makes them feel vulnerable or exposed to criticism (Chapman, Kincaid, Shannon, Schall, & Harrower, in press). The functional assessment interview might yield more complete information once rapport has been established with the family. The family also might be more willing to allow observations within difficult, yet important, contexts once they feel assurance that providers are family centered and supportive.

Hypothesis development. The next step in the process is to develop hypotheses about the problem behavior. These behavioral hypotheses are summary statements of what was learned through the functional assessment information. Hypothesis statements represent the best informed guess about the relation of environmental features to problem behavior and the purposes of problem behavior given the functional assessment information. The hypothesis statements are the foundation for building the behavior support plan. An examination of the hypothesis statements reveals what skill the child will need to learn to replace the problem behavior. The goal of the support plan will be to create conditions that make the problem behavior unnecessary and ineffective for the child (Dunlap, Vaughn, & O'Neill, 1998; O'Neill et al., 1997). This is accomplished by teaching the child a skill that is the functional equivalent of the problem behavior (i.e., results in achieving the same outcome) and removing the reinforcer for the problem behavior. In addition, prevention or antecedent strategies are developed to provide the child with adjustments in the environment, activities, and events that reduce the need for the child to use problem behavior to achieve a goal (Dunlap et al., 1998; O'Neill et al., 1997).

It is important that the professional who works with the family in the analysis of functional assessment information and the development of the hypotheses statements maintains sensitivity as to how the family might react to the information presented. Discussions about how behaviors are maintained must be presented carefully so that the parents do not feel that they have done something "wrong." It is important that the parent understands how problem behaviors are based communicatively and how their response might maintain behavior but also that their child's development of conventional communication skills can be shaped with purposeful intervention.

Functional analysis. When there is ambiguity about the purpose of behavior, a functional analysis might be used to confirm a hypothesis or identify clear patterns regarding the predictors and consequences associated with problem behavior (O'Neill et al., 1997). In a functional analysis, variables in the environment are manipulated to test the hypothesized functions of problem behavior. Thus, functional analyses typically require the use of single-subject research designs and are conducted within controlled settings. However, the case can be made that the use of formal functional analysis procedures with young children is rarely necessary because their behaviors are less complex and their learning histories are relatively brief (Dunlap & Fox, 1996; Dunlap et al., 1990; Weigle, 2000). Thus, a functional analysis might add a time-consuming and unnecessary step to the process.

COMPREHENSIVE EARLY INTERVENTION

In positive behavioral support, researchers have called for comprehensive applications of an assessment-based approach to behavior intervention (Carr et al., 1994; Fox, Vaughn, et al., 1997; Horner & Carr, 1997; Meyer & Evans, 1989). Interventions are comprehensive when they (a) are based on a functional assessment of problem behavior; (b) address all problem behaviors; (c) utilize multiple intervention procedures; (d) apply these procedures throughout the day; and (e) are consistent with the values and resources of the persons providing, and being provided with, behavioral support (Horner & Carr, 1997). The goal of positive behavioral support is to achieve important lifestyle outcomes for the child with challenging behavior. Those outcomes are determined individually but might include accessing new environments and activities as well as developing meaningful and reciprocal social relationships. These outcomes are ambitious and only likely to be achieved through a sustained effort of behavioral support that is applied in all environments by the individuals who are most likely to interact with the child with challenging behavior.

Developing the Plan

The development of a behavior support plan with the family to address a child's problem behavior is a vital step in the provision of comprehensive, assessment-based intervention. Based on the hypotheses developed from the functional assessment information, strategies and modifications in the environment are identified that might reduce the likelihood that the child will use problem behavior (Luiselli & Cameron, 1998). When setting events have been identified that might impact problem behavior, strategies should be developed to address those issues. For example, if a child has more problem behavior at preschool when he or she has skipped eating breakfast, he or she might be offered breakfast on arrival at preschool. Or, if a child is more difficult following a night without sleep, strategies that will help the child settle down for sleep (e.g., decreasing caffeine in the evening, establishing a consistent bedtime routine) might be included in the support plan.

In addition to making modifications in the child's environment, replacement skills are identified that match the identified purpose of the problem behavior or will result in the same outcome as the problem behavior. In selecting the replacement skill or functional equivalent to the problem behavior, it is critical that the replacement skill that is selected will be easy for the child to perform and readily interpretable (and responded to) by others in the environment. Recently, researchers have found that teaching functionally equivalent replacement skills not only increases young children's use of appropriate behavior but also appears to prevent minor problem behaviors from escalating to more serious ones (Reeve & Carr, in press).

While ensuring that children receive access to desired reinforcement when they do engage in positive behavior, the support plan also must provide instructions for how adults will react to problem behavior when it occurs. It is important that strategies are outlined that guide adults in responding to problem behavior in ways that make the behavior ineffective (O'Neill et al., 1997). If the problem behavior is not severe, its occurrence might be treated as an instructional opportunity in which the child might be guided to use the replacement skill (Dunlap et al., 1998), although instructional situations where a child is upset are not the most effective. When incorporating these strategies into a comprehensive plan, it is important that the replacement skills are taught throughout the day and within a variety of natural situations (L. K. Koegel, Koegel, Harrower, & Carter, 1999).

The final component of the development of a behavior support plan is to come up with long-term support strategies that address lifestyle considerations. Although it might seem unusual to think about a young child's lifestyle, children with severe problem behavior and their families often have very restricted lives (Turnbull & Ruef, 1996). When children display significant problem behavior, they, and thus their families, are often excluded from engaging in the same activities as peers without such behavior and their families. It is important that children with challenging behavior and their families are supported in building the kind of lifestyle they would envision if their children did not experience behavior problems.

Implementing and Monitoring Outcomes

The development of a technically sound behavior support plan provides a framework for comprehensive, assessment-based intervention. The behavior support plan will include many ways that adults will change what they do to support and respond to the child with problem behavior. This ongoing stage of the process requires that team members specifically collaborate on how the plan will be implemented and monitored. First, the team must work together to ensure that the plan is implemented with consistency and effective in achieving their goals. Furthermore, the team (a) identifies the training and resources needed, (b) determines who is responsible for monitoring implementation, (c) evaluates outcomes (through continued data collection), and (d) communicates periodically, making adjustments in the plan, as needed. The interventionist will need to work closely with the family and other care providers to facilitate their use of these strategies and the modification of their interactions with the child.

Ensuring Contextual Fit

It is essential that the behavior support plan be designed in such a way that the family and other care providers can implement strategies in all of the child's routines and environments. The concept of contextual fit has been described as the design of behavior support plans that are compatible with the individual for whom the plan is designed, with the people implementing the plan, and with the environment in which the plan will be implemented (Albin et al., 1996). When the contextual fit of a support plan is good, the plan will be implemented with fidelity. If the contextual fit is poor, the plan might not be implemented consistently and behavior change will not result. From this perspective, attention to contextual fit has been a key element in successful applications of comprehensive behavioral support with families and their children with severe problem behavior (Fox, Vaughn, et al., 1997; Lucyshyn, Albin, & Nixon, 1997; Vaughn, Dunlap, Fox, Clarke, & Bucy, 1997).

The concept of contextual fit recognizes the critical importance of understanding the broader ecology of the child in the application of positive behavioral support. It is possible to develop a behavior support plan that is technically sound but does not fit with the values, routines, and lifestyle patterns of the family (Albin et al., 1996). The development of a plan with contextual fit requires the acknowledgment of the important roles the family and other caregivers have in the development and implementation of the behavior support plan. Once again, an effective person-centered planning process will help to identify many of those issues affecting the child and the ecology of the family system. As a result, person-centered planning might provide information critical to the contextual fit of the support plan. Building on this foundation, interventionists then can work in partnership with families in identifying strategies that will be effective in reducing problem behavior and teaching the child new skills that "fit" the family context. Furthermore, strategies are to be developed that are effective and feasible for implementation by all of the persons who interact with the child.

NICKY: A CASE STUDY

Nicky was a 26-month-old child diagnosed with pervasive developmental disorder who lived with his father, mother, older brother, and infant sister. He was provided with speech and language therapy, occupational therapy, and specialized instruction within his home by the local Part C provider. Nicky had prolonged tantrums that were highly disruptive to his family life and interfered with the ability to be engaged with his therapist and early interventionist. Nicky would not follow an adult's direction, reacted to self-care routines (bathing, diaper changing) with prolonged tantrums, had difficulty leaving and returning home, and protested by having tantrums when others joined his play activities. Nicky's family said they felt that they were unable to impose any demands on him and had greatly restructured their family life to avoid triggering his problem behavior.

The early intervention team implemented the behavior support process by first dividing responsibility for information gathering through functional assessment. The early interventionist used a functional assessment interview with the family to define the problem behaviors and identify the possible triggers and maintaining variables associated with Nicky's problem behavior. In addition, the early interventionist and occupational therapist conducted observations within routines identified by the family as problematic. The speech therapist conducted an informal communication and play assessment to contribute information on Nicky's strengths and instructional needs. The family also was provided with observation cards to note the antecedents and consequences to Nicky's problem behavior when it occurred.

The entire team, including Nicky's parents, met to review the information and identify patterns in Nicky's behavior. The team was able to determine that Nicky used tantrums to escape the demands of difficult play activities (i.e., play involving turn taking or complex action schemes) and self-care routines. When he had tantrums, adults removed the demand or stopped interacting with him. Nicky also had tantrums when transitions occurred, even when the transition was to a more desirable activity. Often, when Nicky tantrummed during a transition, the adult delayed or dropped the transition.

In addition to the review of the functional assessment information, the team conducted a person-centered planning meeting. The person-centered planning meeting included the entire family, the early interventionist, the therapist, Nicky's grandmother, and Nicky's godmother. The person-centered planning meeting was the first time that Nicky's family gathered to discuss their commitment to supporting Nicky and their dreams for his future. In the person-centered planning meeting, the circle of support identified the following as important goals for Nicky's future: (a) developing more play skills, (b) communicating, (c) becoming independent in self-care, (d) meeting friends in the community, and (e) going to school.

A behavior support plan was developed for Nicky that included steps to achieve the goals identified in the person-centered plan and teach him skills that would replace his problem behavior. His behavior support plan included long-term support strategies, prevention strategies, replacement skill instruction, and ways to respond to the problem behavior when it occurred. The long-term support strategies included providing Nicky with a predictable activity schedule that included outdoor play and community experiences, inviting children over to play with Nicky, and teaching Nicky to be independent in self-care routines. Strategies to prevent the occurrence of problem behavior included using a visual schedule to inform Nicky of activities and choices, offering Nicky choices within activities and routines, using transition signals, simplifying language input and pairing prompts with visual symbols or gestures, and embedding turn taking within difficult routines and play activities. Nicky was taught to use his visual schedule and choice boards to make requests and was taught to gesture a protest or "no" in response to choices. In addition, play routines and activities were structured to teach Nicky to tolerate simple social exchanges. Finally, strategies for responding to Nicky's problem behavior included following through with a demands that were given to Nicky, offering help to Nicky to complete one step of an activity routine before allowing escape, responding to Nicky's protest by labeling the message (e.g., "You don't want to go in the car"), and calmly guiding him through the activity.

Nicky's behavior support plan was implemented by his early intervention team and his family. The early interventionist modeled for the family how to use each of the strategies and provided the family with feedback when observing their interactions with Nicky. The speech therapist developed Nicky's visual schedule and assisted the family in refining the schedule and developing additional visual supports for Nicky. Everyone who interacted with Nicky (including the family) used a communication notebook to comment on how Nicky was responding to the behavior support plan and tracked his progress in skill acquisition and problem behavior reduction.

At age 3, Nicky was able to transition to a preschool classroom at his elementary school. A transition meeting was held prior to his attending school to share the most recent version of his behavior support plan and discuss important strategies for ensuring a smooth transition. His tantrums were minimal, and he adjusted quickly to his new environment, therapists, and teachers.

ADDITIONAL CONSIDERATIONS

Having outlined a process for functional assessment and comprehensive early intervention, we now turn to a discussion regarding three issues of particular relevance to the process as it relates specifically to early intervention. These three issues include effectively involving families, utilizing collaborative teaming, and implementing intervention in multiple contexts and are each essential to comprehensive early intervention.

Family Involvement

The practice of involving families in the process of functional assessment and positive behavioral support for young children with challenges in behavioral adaptation is extremely important. The impact of challenging behavior on family life can be highly disruptive and pervasive, affecting all family members and family lifestyle (Turnbull & Ruef, 1996). Positive behavioral support is a comprehensive approach that can be arranged to benefit the full family system. The general rationale and importance of family involvement in young children's educational and support programs has been articulated in many ways and in many places (e.g., Division of Early Childhood, 1999; Dunlap, Newton, Fox, Benito, & Vaughn, in press; Dunst, 1997; L. K. Koegel et al., 1999).

In comparison to teachers and other professionals, families almost always possess the greatest amount of information about their child. Family members typically spend an extensive number of hours with their child, and they have the benefit of having observed and interacted with him or her on a daily basis for years. It is also typical that family members have gained special insights into many aspects of their child's behavior that are extremely relevant for a functional assessment. In addition, because young children with significant behavioral challenges usually bring extended and intensive caregiving responsibilities, many families are invested heavily in the behavioral support process. The presence of significant problem behaviors creates a great impact on families' functioning (Fox, Vaughn, et al., 1997), and, therefore, families often are deeply concerned with finding practical "real life" solutions.

Fortunately, there is a current trend in the literature toward specifically addressing family involvement, as well as including family members as partners in the process of functional assessment and positive behavior support (Lucyshyn, Dunlap, & Albin, in press). Family members have been shown to be effective informants, data collectors, and intervention agents in home and community contexts (Derby et al., 1997; Vaughn, Clarke, & Dunlap, 1997; Wacker, Cooper, Peck, Derby, & Berg, 1999). Research has further shown that parents can be successful at generating and testing hypotheses regarding the functions of the problem behaviors of their children (Arndorfer, Miltenberger, Woster, Rortvedt, & Gaffaney, 1994) as well as effectively teaching appropriate replacement behaviors based on the functional assessment information they gather (Frea & Hepburn, 1999). Additional reports are describing significant involvement on the part of family members in the processes of functional assessment and positive behavior support (e.g., Boulware, Schwartz, & McBride, 1999; Moes & Frea, 2000). A family-centered model of early intervention relies on the premise that parents will gain expertise and confidence in conducting functional assessments and developing assessment-based interventions for their children (Dunlap & Fox, 1996, 1999a; Fox, Benito, & Dunlap, in press; Fox, Dunlap, & Philbrick, 1997). The expectation with this model is that parents will come to possess the problem-solving and team membership skills that will enable them to maintain an active involvement (and leadership) throughout the many years of their children's development.

Early intervention efforts must recognize the critical need to provide supports that serve to strengthen and sustain the family system. Dunlap and Fox (1999b) described three issues in this area of family support that deserve special attention. First, professionals should strive to enhance family competence and confidence. This includes enhancing skills in promoting the development of the child as well as increasing the families' familiarity with the availability of, and process for accessing, relevant services. Second, early intervention efforts should address support from a lifestyle perspective. Thus, by incorporating intervention strategies (whereby individual family members are able to maintain ongoing daily routines that consist of their preferences, values, and ambitions), the likelihood of success can be increased dramatically. Finally, early intervention efforts should arrange for stability and continuity in support relationships. This is an especially important issue in the area of early intervention. Once a child turns 3 years old, the family-centered services mandated by Part C of IDEA end, and the child's services are described in educational terms offered under the provisions of Part B of IDEA. Without the family-centered orientation in Part C of IDEA, families can find themselves without family support resources, resulting in a difficult transitional period in determining the next round of intervention services. Thus, there exists a current need to provide families with stable, ongoing, and supportive relationships with professionals to ensure smooth transitions in a family's ongoing access to appropriate intervention and support. Furthermore, it is essential that families are encouraged and allowed to take on advocacy and leadership roles with regard to their child's services.

Collaborative Teaming

Although collaborative teaming generally is recognized as an essential component of the positive behavioral support process (Dunlap et al., 2000), it is particularly necessary when designing and implementing comprehensive early intervention. Recent research supports the development of comprehensive intervention from an interdisciplinary and collaborative team approach that promotes family-professional partnerships (Fox, Vaughn, et al., 1997; Vaughn, Dunlap, et al., 1997). Collaborative teaming can increase the probability that services will be coördinated, and interventions will be comprehensive and integrated, both issues of extreme importance to early intervention. Furthermore, when interdisciplinary teams work together for a common goal, they increase their potential to promote broad, durable changes in a child's behavior (Hieneman & Dunlap, 1999). Positive behavioral support is enhanced by the development of partnerships with the persons who are most intimately involved with the individual who is displaying problem behavior (Albin et al., 1996). Thus, positive behavioral support explicitly incorporates collaborative teaming in its development and implementation.

The construction of a collaborative team can be particularly challenging when the child is receiving early intervention in a variety of environments by a variety of providers. It is critically important that one person serve as a facilitator of the teaming process with an intention to involve all the child's providers. In addition, it will be important that the teaming process is welcoming to child care providers as well as the early intervention professionals. The success of the behavior support effort hinges on the application of the plan with integrity in all of the child's environments.

Implementing Intervention Across Environments

Just as assessment information is to be gathered in multiple contexts, for intervention to be comprehensive it too must be implemented across environments. Again, this is particularly important when designing supports for young children. The 1997 amendments to IDEA charge early interventionists with the responsibility to move beyond applying intervention in environments that were designed to meet special needs and provide services in "natural environments, including the home, and community settings in which children without disabilities participate" (Pub. L. 105–117, 20 U.S.C. § 1401 *et seq.* (1997)). A sampling of environments where intervention might need to be implemented for young children includes preschool programs, child care centers, parties and outings with peers, shopping centers, parks, restaurants, churches, museums, and friends' houses. Providing early intervention in natural, multiple environments is important as it increases the likelihood that children will generalize skills across settings. It also allows children increased opportunity to practice newly learned skills as well as to imitate and participate in play activities, verbal exchanges, and social interactions with their typically developing peers.

Implementation across natural environments will require that the functional assessment process considers all of the child's environments and activity routines and that a comprehensive support plan will be developed that can be implemented in those environments. This might pose a challenge for early intervention teams who are accustomed to working in more traditional settings (e.g., child care, home, etc.) and at traditional hours. To develop a fruitful functional assessment and effective comprehensive support plan, professionals will have to be willing to conduct observations and provide support in new environments (e.g., shopping center, playground) and at times of the day when the family and child need support (e.g., dinner, bath).

SUMMARY AND CONCLUSIONS

In this article we have attempted to stress the importance of some core elements when utilizing functional assessment with young children displaying problem behavior. We emphasize the importance of involving families in the process in a way that is fully respectful of each family as an individual system characterized by idiosyncratic values, ambitions, interests, strengths, and challenges. In addition, each family that includes a young child with behavioral challenges experiences significant needs, and although there are commonalties, these needs differ from family to family and usually include identifiable concerns that span the areas of informational, social, and emotional support (Turnbull & Turnbull, 1996). Because families are by far the most essential resource available for their children, the ultimate effectiveness of early intervention corresponds directly to the extent that families can be supported in their efforts to maintain a cohesive, nurturing, and positive familial context. Therefore, it is essential that early interventionists adopt a comprehensive and individually responsive approach to family support to ensure that the different kinds of needs a family experiences can be addressed in a sensitive and meaningful manner.

Within the last few years, there has been a significant increase in the number of effective indirect and direct methods for determining why a child is exhibiting challenging behavior. In addition, these methods are being adapted and applied in such a way as to be responsive to a family's strengths and existing support systems. As a result, families are being supported in developing collaborations with professionals and interventionists in conducting functional assessments, developing hypotheses, and designing and implementing positive behavior support interventions.

Finally, although contextual fit issues in positive behavioral support are important in all environments and across individuals of all ages, they are critically important in the context of family life. Positive behavioral support approaches are not so much about changing the behavior of a child as changing the behavior of families and interventionists supporting the child. A technically sound behavior support plan will be most effective if developed through collaborative teaming of parents, professionals, and other caregivers. The resulting behavioral support plan will be more efficient and effective because it will address issues important to not only an individual child but also his or her family. As a result, desirable quality of life outcomes are likely to be achieved by not only the child but also the family.

As we begin to apply what we have learned about supporting families, functional assessment and behavioral support plans are no longer being seen as activities that happen to a family but are developed in complete collaboration with a family. Families have always had the central role of educating, caring for, and nurturing their children. In the framework of a positive behavior support process, families are also taking appropriate collaborative leadership roles in all aspects of the behavioral support process for their child with challenging behaviors. This recognition of the primary role of family members in the positive behavioral support process will continue to have a tremendous impact on the quality of life of individual families and valued outcomes for individual children. Furthermore, this recognition will shape and direct the way positive behavioral interventions are developed, applied, and evaluated in the future.

ACKNOWLEDGMENTS

This article was supported in part by U.S. Department of Education Grant No. H326S980003. The opinions expressed herein do not necessarily reflect the position or policy of the Department, and no official endorsement by the Department should be inferred.

REFERENCES

Albin, R. W., Lucyshyn, J. M., Horner, R. H., & Flannery, K. B. (1996). Contextual fit for behavioral support plans. In L. K. Koegel, R. L. Koegel, & G. Dunlap (Eds.), *Positive behavioral support: Including people with difficult behavior in the community* (pp. 81–98). Baltimore: Brookes.

Arndorfer, R. E., Miltenberger, R. G., Woster, S. H., Rortvedt, A. K., & Gaffaney, T. (1994). Home-based descriptive and experimental analysis of problem behaviors in children. *Topics in Early Childhood Special Education, 14*(1), 64–87.

Bambara, L. M., & Knoster, T. (1998). *Designing positive behavior support plans*. Washington, DC: American Association on Mental Retardation.

Boulware, G. L., Schwartz, I., & McBride, B. (1999). Addressing challenging behaviors at home: Working with families to find solutions. *Young Exceptional Children, 3,* 21–27.

Carr, E. G., Horner, R. H., Turnbull, A., Marquis, J., Magito-McLaughlin, D., McAtee, M., Smith, C. E., Anderson-Ryand, K. A., Ruef, M., & Doolabh, A. (1999). Positive behavior support as an approach for dealing with problem behavior in people with developmental disabilities: A research synthesis. *American Association on Mental Retardation Monograph.*

Carr, E. G., Levin, L., McConnachie, G., Carlson, J. I., Kemp, D. C., & Smith, C. E. (1994). *Communication-based interventions for problem behavior: A user's guide for producing behavior change*. Baltimore: Brookes.

Chapman, C., Kincaid, D. K., Shannon, P., Schall, C., & Harrower, J. K. (in press). It's about us: Families and positive behavior support. In J. M. Lucyshyn, G. Dunlap, & R. W. Albin (Eds.), *Families, family life, and positive behavior support: Addressing the challenge of problem behaviors in family contexts*. Baltimore: Brookes.

Dadson, S., & Horner, R. H. (1993). Manipulating setting events to decrease problem behaviors: A case study. *Teaching Exceptional Children, 25*(1), 53–55.

Derby, K. M., Wacker, D. P., Berg, W., DeRaad, A., Ulrich, S., Asmus, J., Harding, J., Prouty, A., Laffey, P., & Stoner, E. (1997). The long-term effects of functional communication training in home settings. *Journal of Applied Behavior Analysis, 30,* 507–531.

Division of Early Childhood. (1999). *Concept paper on the identification of and intervention with challenging behavior*. Reston, VA: Author.

Dunlap, G., & Fox, L. (1996). Early intervention and serious problem behaviors: A comprehensive approach. In L. K. Koegel, R. L. Koegel, & G. Dunlap (Eds.), *Positive behavioral support: Including people with difficult behavior in the community* (pp. 31–50). Baltimore: Brookes.

Dunlap, G., & Fox, L. (1999a). A demonstration of behavioral support for young children with autism. *Journal of Positive Behavior Interventions, 1*(2), 77–87.

Dunlap, G., & Fox, L. (1999b). Supporting families of young children with autism. *Infants and Young Children, 12,* 48–54.

Dunlap, G., Hieneman, M., Knoster, T., Fox, L., Anderson, J., & Albin, R. W. (2000). Essential elements of inservice training in positive behavior support. *Journal of Positive Behavior Interventions, 2*(1), 22–32.

Dunlap, G., Johnson, L. F., & Robbins, F. (1990). Preventing serious behavior problems through skill development and early intervention. In A. C. Repp & N. N. Singh (Eds.), *Perspectives on the use of nonaversive and aversive interventions for persons with developmental disabilities* (pp. 273–286). New York: Sycamore.

Dunlap, G., Newton, S., Fox, L., Benito, N., & Vaughn, B. (in press). Family involvement in functional assessment and positive behavior support. *Focus on Autism.*

Dunlap, G., Vaughn, B. J., & O'Neill, R. E. (1998). Comprehensive behavioral support: Application and intervention. In A. M. Wetherby, S. F. Warren, & J. Reichle (Eds.), *Transitions in prelinguistic communication* (pp. 343–364). Baltimore: Brookes.

Dunst, C. J. (1997). Conceptual and empirical foundations of family-centered practice. In R. J. H. Illback & C. T. Cobb (Eds.), *Integrated services for children and families: Opportunities for psychological practice* (pp. 75–91). Washington, DC: American Psychological Association.

Forest, M., & Lusthaus, E. (1987). The kaleidoscope: Challenge to the cascade. In M. Forest (Ed.), *More education/integration* (pp. 1–16). Ontario, Canada: G. Allan Roeher Institute.

Foster-Johnson, L., & Dunlap, G. (1993). Using functional assessment to develop effective, individualized interventions. *Teaching Exceptional Children, 25,* 44–50.

Fox, L., Benito, N., & Dunlap, G. (in press). Early intervention with families of young children with autism spectrum disorder and problem behavior. In J. M. Lucyshyn, G. Dunlap, & R. W. Albin (Eds.), *Families, family life, and positive behavioral support: Addressing the challenge of problem behavior in family contexts.* Baltimore: Brookes.

Fox, L., Dunlap, G., & Buschbacher, P. (in press). Understanding and intervening with young children's problem behavior: A comprehensive approach. In A. M. Wetherby & B. M. Prizant (Eds.), *Communication and language issues in autism and pervasive developmental disorder: A transactional developmental perspective.* Baltimore: Brookes.

Fox, L., Dunlap, G., & Philbrick, L. A. (1997). Providing individualized supports to young children with autism and their families. *Journal of Early Intervention, 21,* 1–14.

Fox, L., Vaughn, B. J., Dunlap, G., & Bucy, M. (1997). Parent–professional partnership in behavioral support: A qualitative analysis of one family's experience. *The Journal of the Association for Persons With Severe Handicaps, 22,* 198–207.

Frea, W. D., & Hepburn, S. L. (1999). Teaching parents of children with autism to perform functional assessments to plan interventions for extremely disruptive behaviors. *Journal of Positive Behavior Interventions, 1,* 112–116.

Hieneman, M., & Dunlap, G. (1999). Issues and challenges in implementing community- based support for two boys with severe behavioral difficulties. In J. R. Scotti & L. H. Meyer (Eds.), *Behavioral intervention: Principles, models, and practices* (pp. 363–384). Baltimore: Brookes.

Horner, R. H., & Carr, E. G. (1997). Behavioral support for students with severe disabilities: Functional assessment and comprehensive intervention. *The Journal of Special Education, 31,* 84–104.

Horner, R. H., O'Neill, R. E., & Flannery, K. B. (1993). Building effective behavior support plans from functional assessment information. In M. E. Snell (Ed.), *Systematic instruction for students with severe handicaps* (4th ed., pp. 184–214). Columbus, OH: Merrill.

Individuals With Disabilities Education Act Amendments of 1997, 20 U. S. C. § 1400 *et seq.* (1997).

Kennedy, C. H., & Itkonen, T. (1993). Effects of setting events on the problem behavior of students with severe disabilities. *Journal of Applied Behavior Analysis, 26,* 321–327.

Koegel, L. K., Koegel, R. L., & Dunlap, G. (Eds.). (1996). *Positive behavioral support: Including people with difficult behavior in the community.* Baltimore: Brookes.

Koegel, L. K., Koegel, R. L., Harrower, J. K., & Carter, C. M. (1999). Pivotal response intervention I: Overview of approach. *Journal of the Association for Persons With Severe Handicaps, 24,* 174–185.

Koegel, R. L., Koegel, L. K., & Surratt, A. V. (1992). Language intervention and disruptive behavior in preschool children with autism. *Journal of Autism and Developmental Disorders, 22,* 141–153.

Lucyshyn, J. M., Albin, R. W., & Nixon, C. D. (1997). Embedding comprehensive behavioral support in family ecology: An experimental, single-case analysis. *Journal of Consulting and Clinical Psychology, 65,* 241–251.

Lucyshyn, J. M., Dunlap, G., & Albin, R. W. (Eds.). (in press). *Families, family life, and positive behavior support: Addressing the challenge of problem behaviors in family contexts.* Baltimore: Brookes.

Luiselli, J. K., & Cameron, M. J. (Eds.). (1998). *Antecedent control: Innovative approaches to behavioral support.* Baltimore: Brookes.

McEvoy, M. A., Nordquist, V. M., Twardosz, S., Heckaman, K., Wehby, J. H., & Denny, R. K. (1988). Promoting autistic children's peer interaction in an integrated early childhood setting using affection activities. *Journal of Applied Behavior Analysis, 21,* 193–200.

Meyer, L. H., & Evans, I. M. (1989). *Nonaversive intervention for behavior problems: A manual for home and community.* Baltimore: Brookes.

Moes, D. R., & Frea, W. D. (2000). Using family context to inform intervention planning for the treatment of a child with autism. *Journal of Positive Behavior Interventions, 2*(1), 40–46.

Mount, B., & Zwernick, K. (1988). *It's never too early it's never too late.* St. Paul, MN: Metropolitan Council.

O'Brien, J., O'Brien, L., & Mount, B. (1997). Person-centered planning has arrived ... or has it? *Mental Retardation, 35,* 480–488.

O'Neill, R. E., Horner, R. H., Albin, R. W., Storey, K., Sprague, J. R., & Newton, J. S. (1997). *Functional assessment of problem behavior: A practical assessment guide.* Pacific Grove, CA: Brooks/Cole.

O'Neill, R. E., Vaughn, B. J., & Dunlap, G. (1998). Comprehensive behavioral support: Assessment issues and strategies. In A. M. Wetherby, S. F. Warren, & J. Reichle (Eds.), *Transitions in prelinguistic communication* (pp. 313–341). Baltimore: Brookes.

Reeve, C. E., & Carr, E. G. (in press). Prevention of severe behavior problems in children with developmental disorders. *Journal of Positive Behavior Interventions.*

Rehabilitation Research & Training Center on Positive Behavioral Support. (2000). *Definition of positive behavioral support.* Retrieved September 25, 2000 from the World Wide Web: http://rrtcpbs.org

Repp, A. C., & Horner, R. H. (Eds.). (1999). *Functional analysis of problem behavior: From effective assessment to effective support.* Belmont, CA: Wadsworth.

Sugai, G., Horner, R. H., Dunlap, G., Hieneman, M., Lewis, T. J., Nelson, C. M., Scott, T., Liaupsin, C., Sailor, W., Turnbull, A. P., Turnbull, H. R., Wickham, D., Wilcox, B., & Ruef, M. (in press). Applying positive behavioral support and functional behavioral assessment in schools. *Journal of Positive Behavior Interventions.*

Tilly, W. D., Knoster, T. P., Kovaleski, J., Bambara, L., Dunlap, G., & Kincaid, D. (1998). *Functional behavioral assessment: Policy development in light of emerging research and practice.* Alexandria, VA: National Association of State Directors of Special Education.

Turnbull, A. P., & Ruef, M. (1996). Family perspectives on problem behavior. *Mental Retardation, 34,* 280–293.

Turnbull, A. P., & Turnbull, H. R. (1996). Group action planning as a strategy for providing comprehensive family support. In L. K. Koegel, R. L. Koegel, & G. Dunlap (Eds.), *Positive behavioral support: Including people with difficult behavior in the community* (pp. 99–114). Baltimore: Brookes.

Vaughn, B. J., Clarke, S., & Dunlap, G. (1997). Assessment-based intervention for severe behavior problems in a natural family context. *Journal of Applied Behavior Analysis, 30,* 713–716.

Vaughn, B. J., Dunlap, G., Fox, L., Clarke, S., & Bucy, M. (1997). Parent–professional partnership in behavioral support: A case study of community-based intervention. *The Journal of the Association for Persons With Severe Handicaps, 22,* 186–197.

Wacker, D. P., Cooper, L. J., Peck, S. M., Derby, K. M., & Berg, W. K. (1999). Community-based functional assessment. In A. C. Repp & R. H. Horner (Eds.), *Functional analysis of problem behavior: From effective assessment to effective support* (pp. 32–56). Belmont, CA: Wadsworth.

Weigle, K. (2000). *Functional analysis: An application to mother–infant interactions.* Unpublished doctoral dissertation, West Virginia University, Morgantown.

EXCEPTIONALITY, *8*(3), 205–215

Elements of Behavior Support Plans: A Technical Brief

Robert H. Horner, George Sugai, Anne W. Todd, and Teri Lewis-Palmer

Department of Special Education
University of Oregon

In their efforts to address challenging problem behaviors, educators and families have indicated a great need to develop and implement effective behavior support plans (BSPs). Fortunately, the functional behavioral assessment technology provides an excellent base for building behavior intervention plans. However, educators and families need guidelines to improve the effectiveness, efficiency, and relevance of the BSPs they develop. The purpose of this article is to review the features of a BSP that teams should consider as they develop effective responses to problem behavior.

As schools struggle to implement the 1997 amendments to the Individuals With Disabilities Education Act (IDEA), interest in defining the key elements of effective behavior support has been renewed. The purpose of this "technical brief" is to review the features of a behavior support plan (BSP) that teams should consider as they develop responses to problem behavior. Our hope is that this article responds especially to the requests from families seeking clarification of what they should look for in a positive BSP developed for their son or daughter. In addition, teachers, special support staff, and administrators should find the guidelines reviewed in this article to be helpful in their efforts to develop effective and relevant BSPs and work collaboratively with families.

We recognize that a comprehensive description of positive behavior support would require a full book and that a number of excellent resources (see References) exist for each of the elements we list. Our focus here is to provide a brief overview with the hope that the reader will explore cited references to gain a more in-depth understanding of relevant elements. To achieve this purpose, we describe the purposes of BSPs and main sec-

Requests for reprints should be sent to Robert Horner, 1235 University of Oregon, Eugene, OR 97403–1235. E-mail: robh@oregon.uorgeon.edu

tions of the BSP: (a) demonstrating an understanding of the problem, (b) redesigning the environment, and (c) organizing for success. In the end, we also provide a simple checklist that includes these elements and is intended to serve as a self-monitoring and self-assessment guide for anyone involved in the development of BSPs.

THE PURPOSES OF BSPS

A BSP defines how an environment will change to help a student reduce problem behaviors, improve prosocial behaviors, and become more successful within the school (Sugai, Horner, et al., 2000). The behavior plan defines what "we" will do differently and how we will know if our efforts to change have been effective in changing student behavior. Behavior plans also are seen as documents that provide professional accountability and increase the consistency with which a team of adults implements a support plan.

Behavior plans typically are developed by a team of individuals who know the student well and are prepared to commit time and resources toward the goal of helping the child change his or her behavior patterns. The team often will include teachers, administrators, specialists, family members, and (in many cases) the student. The information that is needed to guide the development of BSPs is obtained by conducting a functional behavioral assessment (FBA; see Sugai, Horner, & Sprague, 1999; Sugai, Lewis-Palmer, & Hagan, 1998; Sugai, Lewis-Palmer, & Hagan-Burke, 1999–2000/this issue). Together, the FBA and BSP assist the team to (a) demonstrate an understanding of the problem, (b) redesign the environment, and (c) organize for success.

DEMONSTRATING AN UNDERSTANDING OF THE PROBLEM

An effective BSP should begin by defining the extent to which the team understands what is occurring and why problems keep occurring. This section of the plan typically has four parts.

Positive Contributions

A good BSP often begins by defining positive contributions of the student. Effective plans build on the strengths of a student (e.g., enjoys reading and writing science fiction short stories, volunteers at the recycling center, visits with school nurse two to three times a week), and defining what the student brings to the school is a useful way to begin the process of identifying effective solutions (e.g., positive reinforcers, engagement activities).

Operational Definitions

The reason for spending time and effort in the design of behavior support is the belief that this investment will result in behavior change that is in the best interest of the child. An important first step is to agree on all the problem behaviors that currently serve as barriers to effective education and social inclusion for the student. The two most common errors made in defining problem behaviors are (a) to define only one behavior when many are problematic and (b) to describe behaviors as internal states (e.g., angry, mean) or diagnostic categories (autism, attention deficit hyperactivity disorder [ADHD], Asperger syndrome) rather than as observable events (e.g., runs away, does not respond to other-initiated conversations, uses profanity).

It is very important for a team to agree on the exact behaviors that are being targeted. A good definition of problem behavior will allow someone who reads the plan to recognize or record occurrences of the behavior. A poor example of a behavior description would be the following: "Karl is cruel to the other children." On reading that statement, the reader does not know what Karl does that is cruel. A better alternative would be "Karl pushes other children, calls them rude names, and threatens physical violence." A good behavioral definition tells us something about how often it occurs (frequency), where it occurs (locus), what it looks like (topography), how long it occurs (duration), how strong it is (intensity), and how long it takes for it to occur (latency).

A team needs to agree with precision on the full set of problem behaviors that will be the focus of the BSP. A common misrule is to focus on one problem behavior when, in fact, the student displays a number of different behaviors. Some of these behaviors are unrelated and independent of each other (i.e., used only under specific conditions or routines and for specific reasons), are part of behavioral chains (i.e., behavioral escalations), or are members of a response class (i.e., different behaviors that have a similar function). It is important to remember to look at and define all of the problem behaviors that a student displays and then look for similarities and differences among them.

Problem Routines

One of the most important features of effective behavior support is focusing on the context where problem behavior occurs. One effective way to accomplish this focus is to write out the student's daily schedule and rate each daily routine as being more or less likely to be associated with problem behaviors. Routines might be individual classes (e.g. math, art, social science), transitions (arrival, passing periods, lunch), or specific activities (independent seatwork, small-group project time, class lecture). By listing the student's schedule and defining where problems do and do not occur, the team often will identify where additional assessment information is needed (e.g., all classes, times when the team is unclear if the child is having difficulty) and identify where the student is doing well. It is as important to learn where a student is being successful as it is to learn where she or he is having difficulty.

By collecting information about problem behavior, teams will be able to focus the strategies they identify and develop in their BSPs. For example, features of the times and places where the problem behavior is less likely to occur can be built into strategies to inhibit or prevent occurrences of problem behavior or to encourage displays of desirable behavior. Similarly, those conditions that are associated with a high likelihood of problem behavior can be modified to discourage problem behavior and encourage expected behavior. Routine information also can be used to identify specific times and places where the interventions of the BSP should be initiated.

FBA

FBA is a process for identifying the events that reliably predict and maintain problem behaviors (Horner & Carr, 1997; O'Neill et al., 1997). Information from the FBA process is essential for the development of BSPs, and the process typically is led or coordinated by trained special educators, school psychologists, counselors, or specialists with input and collaboration from the behavior support team. The process can occur through a wide array of strategies, but the most common approach is to interview those who know the student best (this also might include interviewing the student) and complete direct observations (or even systematic manipulations of the setting) to confirm the hypotheses that arise from the interviews.

The process might be very simple or in complex situations might require considerable skill and expertise (Repp & Horner, 1999). In all cases, however, a competent FBA will result in (a) operational definitions of problem behavior, (b) identification of the events that reliably predict where problem behaviors are most and least likely, (c) identification of the consequences that are believed to maintain the problem behavior, and (d) some form of direct observation data supporting the hypotheses.

Effective functional assessments often are organized around problem routines and result in a "summary" statement that describes what the student does, the conditions that are likely to trigger the problem behavior, and an assumption or hypothesis about what consequences appear to maintain the behavior. An assessment might conclude that, for example, "When Carla is asked to perform tasks where she is likely to fail, she will whine, complain and be verbally abusive. These behaviors appear to be maintained by escaping the demanding situation." FBAs also result in the collection of direct observation data that help to confirm or refine our confidence in the summary statement. In our example with Carla, "direct observation data collected by the teacher over three days confirmed that 4 of 5 problem instances were consistent with this hypothesis."

If a team takes the time to understand a pattern of problem behavior, they are more likely to build a plan of support that will be both implemented by staff and effective (Carr et al., 1999; Didden, Duker, & Korzilius, 1997). The goal is to use what we learn about the problem behavior and the contexts in which it occurs to construct BSPs that will make the problem behavior less effective and the more desirable replacement behaviors more adaptive and effective for the student.

Redesigning the Environment

Another common misrule is that BSPs are developed to "change" student behavior. Although a change or improvement in student behavior is the ultimate outcome, this change actually is associated with a change in the environment or what the adults (or peers) typically do. Thus, a good behavior plan typically focuses on or defines what adults (or peers) in the environment will do differently to produce a change in the student's behavior.

A tremendous amount has been learned in the past 10 years about how to build effective behavior support in schools. The technology is large and worthy of time and study. This literature can be condensed, however, into a few key elements that should be part of positive BSPs and are described next.

Element 1: Learn how the student perceives or experiences events in his or her environment. A number of disabilities (e.g., ADHD, autism, obsessive–compulsive disorder) alter how a child experiences the world around him or her. It is worth the time to consider and learn about medical, physiological, and social factors that alter how a child is experiencing school. In particular, attention should be focused on factors that might make seemingly neutral events either very positive or very negative for the child (e.g., change in seating arrangement or typical classroom routine, substitute teacher). It is also appropriate for a behavior plan to include identification of the type and level of disability, but this information becomes helpful only if it includes discussion about how these factors affect the student's daily experience and how the BSP might be implemented.

Element 2: Invest in preventing occurrences of problem behavior. A BSP should include strategies that will be implemented *before* problem behaviors occur. The goal is to identify both general and specific features of targeted routines that might reduce the likelihood of problems. For example, changing the way greetings are presented to a student, engaging the student in a successful academic task before presenting a difficult task, asking a student to review a social skill strategy in a situation where it might be used, and so on, could preempt the conditions that encourage problem behavior and create situations that increase the likelihood of more appropriate behavior.

When considering the quality of a BSP, a team should examine "general features" of the classroom, playground, lunchroom, or other locations of problem routines. Research suggests that problems are more likely if the student (a) does not have an effective way to communicate with peers and adults; (b) does not have effective way to move from one place to another; (c) is unable to predict the schedule of events throughout the day; (d) has no choices about what he or she does, with whom, or how long they last; (e) is socially isolated; (f) has access to a limited number of activities; and (g) does not receive positive attention or acknowledgment. This list is long and complex, but the real message is that before intense behavioral interventions are considered, a team should reflect on the extent to which problem environments have these "general" features. Attending to these general features often results in benefits for many students, not just the student for whom the BSP is being considered.

In addition to changing general features to prevent problem behaviors, it also is possible to alter *specific* environmental features that prevent problems, which effective teachers often do as a regular part of how they teach. The changing of seating arrangements to separate students in conflict is a prevention effort. The modification of the reading difficulty of a math assignment to accommodate the reading skills of a low-functioning student is a method of preventing problem behaviors. As a general rule, if a student is identified as engaging in problem behaviors to escape from aversive events (e.g., demands, public performance), one prevention strategy might focus on eliminating or modifying these aversive events so that they are no longer aversive. The goal is not to remove the child from tasks, expectations, or instruction but to look at how those events can be changed so that they are not aversive for the student (Dunlap, Kern-Dunlap, Clarke, & Robbins, 1991; Dunlap, White, Vera, Wilson, & Panacek, 1996).

Similarly, if a child appears to engage in problem behaviors to gain access to denied events (e.g., peer attention, adult recognition), prevention strategies might consist of (a) making that reward more readily available before problem behaviors occur, (b) making access to the reward more predictable, or (c) giving the child choices that lead to that exact outcome. Preventive approaches are not possible in all situations but might be very effective when they are feasible and might be beneficial as one element of a multielement plan of support.

Element 3: Teaching is the most powerful behavior support strategy available in schools. Most BSPs should include an *instructional* objective. We seldom think of teaching new skills as part of behavior support, but recent research suggests that teaching new, adaptive skills is perhaps the single most powerful strategy for producing durable behavior change. Behavior problems might be perceived as either the result of mislearning or a lack of learning (Wolery, Bailey, & Sugai, 1988). If the team has taken time to understand what conditions lead to problem behavior and what maintains the problem behavior, then it often is possible to identify the skills the student needs to learn to be effective without engaging in problem behavior. This might be as simple as teaching a child with poor communication skills how to ask for a "break" or "help," or as complex as teaching skills for self-management and the development of peer social relationships.

The real message is that effective behavior support is not just about defining the consequences that will punish or control problem behaviors, but about teaching the student the skills that will make problem behaviors irrelevant and comparatively inefficient. The student will *not* perform problem behaviors if he or she has a better, socially acceptable way to get what he or she needs—not simply because he or she wants to avoid being punished.

Among the most exciting advances in the past 10 years has been the addition of systematic instruction as a key element in behavior support. Teachers and families should expect to see instructional objectives that relate directly to building appropriate skills as part of positive BSPs. Explicit strategies for teaching prosocial alternative behaviors will become more prevalent and emphasize general case rules about when and how to use alternative behaviors, consideration of the contexts in which the alternative behaviors are required, direct teacher-led social skills instruction (e.g., model–lead–test), informative corrections when social behavior errors occur, and high-frequency positive reinforcement for displays of acceptable and desired alternative behaviors.

Element 4: Avoid rewarding problem behavior. Among the great ironies in behavior support today is the finding that many families and teachers inadvertently *reward* the very behaviors that they find most troubling. This rewarding of problem behaviors might occur by a teacher choosing to say something like "Ok, you can have your way today so the rest of us can finish the assignment" (i.e., positive reinforcement) or via the more subtle process by which children get out of difficult activities by behaving inappropriately (being sent to the office is an excellent way of avoiding difficult work; i.e., negative reinforcement). As a general rule, problem behaviors should not be ignored in schools. Instead, clear consequences for problem behaviors should be applied consistently and immediately. By taking the time to understand what consequences maintain problem behaviors within daily routines, teachers and families often can identify how to avoid inadvertently rewarding problem behaviors.

Research on disruptive and dangerous behavior in schools has identified that in all too many cases, either teachers or peers reliably reward students when they engage in problem behaviors. A good BSP alters the environment so problem behaviors do not result in gaining access to preferred events (e.g., teacher or peer attention or tangible objects or activities) or escape from demanding situations.

Element 5: Reward positive behaviors. Among the first skills that new teachers are taught is that they must create positive environments. However, new teachers often falsely assume that all children look forward to coming to school, being in the class, and interacting with teachers and peers and as a result do not create, build, and implement sufficient positive learning environments. Thus, teachers must establish and sustain classroom and behavior management systems that emphasize the reward of positive behaviors.

One of the major ways that positive environments are established is by providing students with regular acknowledgments for their efforts and success at academic and behavioral tasks. Children must learn to "try," try to learn, and succeed in learning. They must receive positive acknowledgments for engaging in appropriate learning and social skills. These acknowledgments do not need to be artificial, but they need to be valuable, informative, and meaningful for the student. Effective teachers learn and use what is uniquely rewarding for each of their students. When a team has developed an effective BSP, the team has identified what the student finds rewarding and organized the environment so that the student receives this recognition, acknowledgment, reward, or reinforcer on a regular and frequent schedule. The use of positive acknowledgment should be a prominent, dominant, and an obvious feature of the BSP and its implementation.

Children who engage in problem behaviors are at major risk of gaining even less positive attention in school than are other children. Thus, great care and attention should be directed toward organizing effective systems of recognition for children who receive behavior support. In particular, special attention should be given to rewarding those new social and communication skills that have been selected and included in the BSP because they compete with the problem behavior and are more efficient, effective, and relevant for the student than the problem behaviors.

Element 6: Know what to do in the most difficult situations. A good BSP will define with high precision what the staff and family should do if the most extreme problem behavior is displayed by the child. The designers and implementers of a good plan of support should never assume that prevention strategies and efforts to teach and reward alternative behaviors will result in the immediate and total elimination of dangerous and difficult behaviors. In contrast, the assumption always should be that the most extreme behavior a child has done in the past will occur again in the future. If the behavior does not occur, those individuals involved in implementing the plan should be gratified; however, they also must have a very clear understanding of and training for what they should do if problems arise under more extreme situations.

Organizing for Success

A behavior plan is more than a set of procedures; it is an agreement and commitment on how a team will work toward a new level of success for a student. A BSP is incomplete and inadequate if the focus is on containing a student rather than defining how the plan will lead that student toward an effective and successful future. Such a plan takes more than procedures. Careful planning, effective procedures, sustained and accurate implementation, and data-based decision making are required. In addition, organizing for success involves attending to how the BSP will be monitored and adjusted over time and ensuring that the elements of the plan are practical and "doable" in the school or home environment.

Monitoring and evaluation. Individuals who implement a BSP have a professional obligation to monitor the impact of a BSP. Each plan should specify observable outcomes that are monitored and used to assess if the plan is being effective. The evaluation section of the plan should indicate what will be monitored (e.g., frequency of fights, duration of off task) and how often the team will meet to review the evaluation information. The basic message is that most BSPs require modifications, especially in the initial implementation stages when training and time are being organized around a plan. An effective BSP is rarely left unchanged for long time periods; instead, frequent adjustments, deletions, and additions are likely. These modifications can occur in a planful manner, or they might be left to the daily judgment of the staff. Experience suggests that planful monitoring and modification is more effective, especially if information about the student's behavior can be collected and evaluated on a regular basis. The team needs a process to gain the information that will allow modifications in the BSP to be logical and effective (Todd, Horner, Sugai, & Sprague, 1999). Instead of waiting until problems get worse and then reacting to the situation, teams should establish data decision rules that signal a careful examination of the plan because an early indication of problems is suspected.

The contextual fit of BSPs. All too often, teams meet and build BSPs, but the plan becomes only a paper document, not a design for changing real school environment. The best plan will fail if the procedures are not implemented accurately and consistently. It is always important to remember that a BSP is developed and written to guide the actions and behaviors of the implementers of the plan. If the plan is implemented with high fidelity, maximum outcomes for the student are likely. Thus, the development of a BSP should consider the contextual fit between the features of the plan, the skill level and motivation of the implementers of the plan, and the capacity of the environment (e.g., resources, schedule).

Plans often are not implemented because the people who are expected to implement the plan are not involved in the design, are not trained how to implement the plan, do not have the time or resources to do what is written in the plan, and do not believe that the plan will be effective (Albin, Lucyshyn, Horner, & Flannery, 1996). BSPs should be constructed with the direct and active input of the people who will implement the plan. No plan should be developed that is not consistent with the skills, values, resources, and administrative support of those who will implement the plan. This commitment to making sure the plan "fits" the context is seldom emphasized, yet it is essential if the plan is to work. Environments can be altered in many different ways to assist a student to succeed. The goal is to find an approach that is both likely to be effective *and* is likely to be used.

SUMMARY

Our goal has been to provide an overview of elements of BSPs that characterize positive behavior support. We have not emphasized specific procedures or strategies but tried to provide an outline that might be used by school teams as they build plans or by parents as they assess the plans proposed for their children. We recognize that every BSP will not need all of the elements listed to be effective. It might be helpful, however, at least to consider each of the elements as a plan is developed and implemented. Toward that end, Table 1 includes a short checklist that teams and families might find useful as they build and review plans.

TABLE 1
BSP Checklist

Student ________________

When developing and implementing behavior support plans, judge the degree to which each of the following has been considered:

G = Good, O = Okay, P = poor, N = not applicable

		Date
Functional assessment: Develop understanding of problem behavior.	1. Describe problem behavior in operational terms.	
	2. Identify problem routines.	
	3. State complete functional assessment hypothesis.	
	4. Collect data to confirm hypothesis statement.	
Foundations: Consider factors that go across routines.	1. Health and physiology.	
	2. Communication.	
	3. Mobility.	
	4. Predictability.	
	5. Choice.	
	6. Social relationships.	
	7. Activity patterns.	

(*Continued*)

TABLE 1 (Continued)

		Date
Prevention: Make problem behavior irrelevant.	1. Modify activity schedule. 2. Adapt curriculum. 3. Modify design of instruction. 4. Adapt instructional procedures. 5. Add prompts for appropriate behavior. 6. Precorrect for typical problem.	
Teaching: Make problem behavior less efficient.	1. Teach specific replacement skills. 2. Teach adaptive social skills.	
Extinction: Make problem behavior less effective.	1. Minimize positive reinforcement for problem behavior. 2. Minimize negative reinforcement for problem behavior.	
Reinforcement: Make appropriate behavior more effective.	1. Select range of effective positive reinforcers. 2. Maximize schedule of positive reinforcement for appropriate behavior.	
Crisis Intervention Plan: Prevent injury.	1. Arrange environment and practice procedures to prevent crisis and emergency situations. 2. Arrange environment and practice procedures to respond to crisis and emergency situations.	
Ensure Contextual Fit: Match intervention to social and treatment context.	1. Consider values and expectations of adults. 2. Assess skill level and fluency of adults. 3. Determine budget. 4. Assess time requirements. 5. Secure administrative support system. 6. Give priority to best interests of student and family.	
Evaluation and Assessment: Make plan more effective, efficient, and relevant.	1. Specify what questions need to be answered. 2. Specify information to be collected. 3. Develop measurement system. 4. Establish schedule for collecting data. 5. Collect and evaluate data. 6. Use data to improve plan.	

Note. BSP = behavior support plan.

ACKNOWLEDGMENTS

This article was supported in part by U.S. Department of Education Grant No. H326S980003. The opinions expressed herein do not necessarily reflect the position or policy of the Department, and no official endorsement by the Department should be inferred.

REFERENCES

Albin, R. W., Lucyshyn, L. M., Horner, R. H., & Flannery, K. B. (1996). Contextual fit for behavioral support plans: A model for a goodness-of-fit. In L. K. Koegel, R. L. Koegel, & G. Dunlap (Eds.), *Positive behavior support: Including people with difficult behavior in the community* (pp. 81–89). Baltimore: Brookes.

Carr, E. G., Horner, R. H., Turnbull, A. P., Marquis, J. G., McLaughlin, D. M., McAtee, M. L., Smith, C. E., Ryan, K. A., Ruef, M. B., Doolabh, A., & Braddock, D. (1999). *Positive behavior support for people with developmental disabilities: A research synthesis*. Washington, DC: American Association on Mental Retardation.

Didden, R., Duker, P. C., & Korzilius, H. (1997). Meta-analytic study on treatment effectiveness for problem behaviors with individuals who have mental retardation. *American Journal on Mental Retardation, 101,* 387–399.

Dunlap, G., Kern-Dunlap, L., Clarke, S., & Robbins, F. R. (1991). Functional assessment, curricular revisions, and severe behavior problems. *Journal of Applied Behavior Analysis, 24,* 387–397.

Dunlap, G., White, R., Vera, A., Wilson, D., & Panacek, L. (1996). The effects of multi-component, assessment-based curricular modifications on the classroom behavior of children with emotional and behavioral disorders. *Journal of Behavioral Education, 6,* 481–500.

Horner, R. H., & Carr, E. G. (1997). Behavioral support for students with severe disabilities: Functional assessment and comprehensive intervention. *The Journal of Special Education, 31,* 84–104.

Individuals With Disabilities Education Act Amendments of 1997, 20 U.S.C. § 1400 *et seq.* (1997).

O'Neill, R. E., Horner, R. H., Albin, R. W., Sprague, J. R., Storey, K., & Newton, J. S. (1997). *Functional assessment and program development for problem behavior: A practical handbook* (2nd ed.). Pacific Grove, CA: Brooks/Cole.

Repp, A., & Horner, R. H. (Eds.). (1999). *Functional analysis of problem behavior: From effective assessment to effective support.* Belmont, CA: Wadsworth.

Sugai, G., Horner, R. H., & Sprague, J. (1999). Functional assessment-based behavior support planning: Research-to-practice-to-research. *Behavioral Disorders, 24,* 223–227.

Sugai, G., Horner, R. H., Dunlap, G., Hieneman, M., Lewis, T. J., Nelson, C. M., Scott, T., Liaupsin, C., Sailor, W., Turnbull, A. P., Turnbull, H. R., III, Wickham, D., Reuf, M., & Wilcox, B. (2000). Applying positive behavior support and functional behavioral assessment in schools. *Journal of Positive Behavior Interventions and Support, 2*(3), 131–143.

Sugai, G., Lewis-Palmer, T., & Hagan, S. (1998). Using functional assessments to develop behavior support plans. *Preventing School Failure, 43*(1), 6–13.

Sugai, G., Lewis-Palmer, T., & Hagan-Burke, S. (1999–2000/this issue). Overview of the functional behavioral assessment process. *Exceptionality, 8,* 149–160.

Todd, A. W., Horner, R. H., Sugai, G., & Sprague, J. R. (1999). Effective behavior support: Strengthening school-wide systems through a team-based approach. *Effective School Practices, 17*(4), 23–27.

Wolery, M. R., Bailey, D. B., Jr., & Sugai, G. M. (1988). *Effective teaching: Principles and procedures of applied behavior analysis with exceptional students*. Boston: Allyn & Bacon.

EXCEPTIONALITY, *8*(3), 217–230

Using Information Technology to Prepare Personnel to Implement Functional Behavioral Assessment and Positive Behavioral Support

Wayne Sailor, Rachel Freeman, Jody Britten,
Amy McCart, and Christopher Smith
Life Span Institute
University of Kansas

Terry Scott and Mike Nelson
Department of Special Education and Rehabilitation Counseling
University of Kentucky

Reauthorization of the Individuals With Disabilities Education Act (1997) produced new language concerned with placement and instruction of students who present challenging behaviors and for whom there is risk of disability determination. The result is an immediate need for preservice personnel preparation as well as staff and professional development practices and procedures concerned with functional behavioral assessment and positive behavioral support (PBS). Recent advances in information technologies are creating new opportunities for advancing this training agenda. This article examines some of the impediments to effective dissemination of training in PBS such as philosophical barriers, school discipline policies, and the inadequacy of present professional and staff training models. It suggests ways that new information technologies can overcome these obstacles and reviews some new approaches using CD-ROM and online instructional methodologies to advance the training agenda.

The explosion of new information technologies in the past decade has provided a much needed opportunity to reshape the landscape of both personnel training (preservice) and

---

Requests for reprints should be sent to Wayne Sailor, University Affiliated Program–Lawrence, University of Kansas, 1052 Dole Hall, Lawrence, KS 66045. E- mail: w-sailor@ukans.edu

staff development (inservice) in virtually all human services professions and occupations. Historically, practicing teachers initially have had to depend on a knowledge base growing out of the ability of teacher educators to evaluate current research and translate the implications into practice. Once on the job, leaders have had to rely on their own resources and diligence to stay in touch with ongoing research. Lacking resources from university libraries with current journals, new books, and so on, it has been all too common for practicing teachers to fall prey to a well- known lag from research to teaching practice (Gersten, Vaughn, Deshler, & Schiller, in press).

Staff development historically has presented similar challenges. The burden of imparting new research-based information on teaching practices to special education teachers in the field has been borne largely by state departments of education on limited funds provided through the Individuals With Disabilities Education Act (IDEA; 1997) for that purpose. The format for much state approved staff development traditionally has been what has come to be known as "the dog and pony show." Episodic conferences or workshops are held in either the district on a "teacher inservice" day or a central location in the state during the summer months. Experts are brought in to impart new information, group discussions are held, notebooks are issued, and the process is concluded.

There has long been a need for sustained, readily accessible contacts for new research-to- practice materials and information for teacher educators, practicing teachers, and state-level staff development personnel. Information technologies have responded to this need, and the result is a rapidly changing landscape for eliminating the lag from research to practice in special education and other professions. In this article, we focus on the opportunities for new options in teacher education and staff development arising from recent advances in information technology. Our case in point is the critical need to acquaint new, as well as practicing, teachers with the concept and methods of functional behavioral assessment (FBA) and the development of positive behavioral support plans (PBS).

THE CHALLENGE POSED BY IDEA (1997)

New language contained in the reauthorization of the Amendments to the Individuals With Disabilities Act (IDEA) of 1997, which was signed into law on June 4, 1997 has precipitated both crisis and opportunity by creating an immediate, national need for personnel preparation efforts in the areas traditionally concerned with placement and instruction of students who manifest behavioral problems associated with their disabilities or whose behavior places them at risk for disability determination (Turnbull & Ruef, 1996).

The new concepts, to most educators, that have emerged in the statute and have pressing implications for the transfer of research-validated technology into practice (particularly for teachers, service providers in community settings, and families) are PBS and its key operative component, FBA. Section 614 (d)(3)(B)(i) of Pub. L. 105–17 states

> In the case of a child whose behavior impedes his or her learning or that of others, the child's Individual Education Program (IEP) Planning team must consider, when appropriate, strategies, including positive behavioral intervention strategies and supports to address that behavior. (p. 71)

In addition, Section 615(k)(1)(B)(i) of the law states that

> If the local educational agency did not conduct a functional behavioral assessment and implement a behavioral intervention plan for such child before the behavior that resulted in the suspension described in subparagraph (A), the agency shall convene an IEP meeting to develop an assessment plan to address that behavior. (p. 83)

In addition, "if the child already has a behavioral intervention plan, the IEP team shall review the plan and modify it, as necessary, to address the behavior" [Section 615(k)(1)(B)(ii)]. The act also states that

> In response to certain disciplinary actions by school personnel, the IEP team must, within ten days, meet to formulate a functional behavioral assessment plan to collect data for developing a behavior intervention plan, or if a behavior intervention plan already exists, the team must review and revise it (as necessary), to ensure that it addresses the behavior upon which disciplinary action is predicated. (p. 83)

This language is meant to address the issue of a student's potential removal from an educational setting or other change of placement due to suspension or expulsion for reasons of discipline.

A growing body of research demonstrates the effectiveness of PBS and provides specific techniques for reducing problem behavior that do not rely primarily on the use of consequences such as suspension and exclusion (Carr et al., 1999; Durand & Carr, 1991; Kern, Childs, Dunlap, Clarke, & Falke, 1994; Koegel, Koegel, & Dunlap, 1996; Lalli, Browder, Mace, & Brown, 1993; Lewis, Sugai, & Colvin, 1998). Despite the effectiveness of such PBS strategies as FBA, information regarding how to apply research-validated practices in the classroom has not been made available to teachers and other professionals in a format that allows these strategies to become common practice (Anderson, Albin, Mesaros, & Morelli-Robbins, 1993; Nelson, Roberts, Mathur, & Rutherford, 1998; Ruef, Turnbull, Turnbull, & Poston, 1999; Scott & Nelson, 1999a). In fact, one of the most common requests for assistance from teachers is for help in working with students who engage in problem behavior (Horner, Diemer, & Brazeau, 1992).

Traditional professional development models have struggled with a variety of challenges that impede effective dissemination of training in the effective implementation of PBS. Practitioner competencies, philosophical barriers, and school discipline policy issues are but a few of the challenges that impede the ability of schools and community agencies to deliver PBS and FBA information in a manner that is timely and more likely to promote the generalization of newly acquired professional skills. These issues are discussed in the following sections. We conclude by highlighting new formats and strategies for staff development that show promise for the dissemination of effective training in FBA.

IMPEDIMENTS TO IMPLEMENTING FBA

To be effective, schools must embrace the concept of FBA as a common routine whose procedures are adopted, supported, and equally shared across the school (Jolivette,

Barton-Arwood, & Scott, in press; Scott & Nelson, 1999b). Yet, the issues that arise as impediments to school-wide implementation of effective FBA procedures in public schools are not purely training issues. As Scott and Nelson (1999a) suggested, the question of implementation might rely not so much on what is trained and how it is delivered as to whether practitioners are willing to be trained and make changes. History provides us with enough evidence to predict that empirical support and legislation, without practitioner support, will be ineffective in effecting change. We first cover the issues related to practitioner characteristics and competencies, followed by a discussion of the practical barriers to school-wide implementation of effective FBA procedures.

Practitioner Competencies

When queried, teachers report challenging behaviors to be among the most difficult behaviors with which they deal on a daily basis, and they report feeling ill prepared to deal with these problems (Safran & Safran, 1988; Scott, Nelson, & Meers, 1999). Training practitioners to implement FBA is hindered by the fact that many persons lack even basic knowledge of strategies for dealing with problem behaviors. To them, the concept of FBA likely will be too abstract and advanced without exposure to some of the basic applied behavior analysis underpinnings and an understanding of why humans behave. Training in this depth of content is time consuming, complex, and often contrary to the philosophical beliefs of individuals (see next section). Few, if any, of the commercially available training programs in FBA provide a detailed primer in applied behavior analysis.

A second barrier at the personnel level involves individual competencies with collaboration and team decision making. Jolivette, Barton-Arwood, and Scott (in press) identified the following four individual dynamics that might act or interact to set the occasion for collaborative FBA team failure: Team members bring their own (a) unique perspectives of the student and presenting problems, (b) level of expertise with a given problem behavior, (c) agenda and level of commitment that might or might not match those of the group, and (d) working style, which might conflict with the working style of other members.

Again, understanding the process and making it work are two separate issues. It should be clear that simply training FBA as a collaborative process will be insufficient to guarantee effective systemic approaches with those who lack the skills necessary to engage in effective collaboration. If the FBA process is to be effective on a systemic level, training must take into account individual understanding and competencies in the areas of basic behavior modification, applied behavior analysis, and collaboration.

Philosophical Barriers

Because implementation of FBA as part of a school-wide process has implications for all persons in the school, the process can be defined as systemic in nature. Systems change is a dynamic process that involves both practical and philosophical factors (Garmston & Wellman, 1999). As previously noted, effective training must focus not only on the core competencies needed by the personnel involved, but also on their existing belief systems and philosophical orientations.

Because disagreements in this realm often amount to a politically charged debate, it is unlikely that addressing these concerns will change the minds of those truly invested in their philosophy. Rather, training should focus on providing procedural descriptions that incorporate a logically validated rationale, justifying procedures in advance of predictable objections. Clearly, it is unlikely that all persons within a given system will buy into any particular approach, and this will not be a realistic goal. As Sugai and Horner (1999) suggested, 80% faculty consensus to participate seems to be sufficient to predict successful implementation of school-wide processes.

Although the FBA process has a history of use by professionals who work in the area of low- incidence disabilities and with students who exhibit serious behavior problems (e.g., Carr & Durand, 1985; Day, Horner, & O'Neill, 1994; Foster-Johnson & Dunlap, 1993), the newness of this approach in public school programs and with typical and mild disability student populations relegates it to the position of "latest fad" in the minds of those who have seen procedures come and go in education. To avoid falling into this same trap, FBA must be justified rationally and trained using a set of prescriptive guidelines. However, FBA is not a static set of procedures that is used with every student. Rather, it is a dynamic process of inference and decision making, leading to individualized procedures that are based on the unique behaviors and contexts that surround individual students. Although the precise set of procedures likely will vary by individual student, the process must maintain a fidelity of implementation sufficient to maximize the probability of successful outcomes.

However, a recent national survey indicates that experts in the field of mild disabilities do not agree on the specific procedures that are necessary and sufficient to constitute best practice in conducting FBA with this population (Scott, Meers, & Nelson, in press). Without consistent leadership, it seems ridiculous to assume that practitioners will be able to implement FBA with the fidelity necessary to produce systemwide meaningful outcomes. Under these conditions, it seems likely that FBA will follow other education fads into obscurity due to an inability to demonstrate efficiency and utility for schools. However, the questions that arise in FBA are empirical in nature and must be answered as a first priority. As Sugai, Horner, and Sprague (1999) so justifiably advocated, "it is imperative that researchers consolidate what is already known, translate their findings into applications for real-world contexts, and continue to extend the conceptual and applied knowledge base" (p. 256). If FBA is to be effectively trained and implemented on a school-wide basis, we must heed the admonition to continue to extend the research base to create the prescriptive guidelines necessary to facilitate reliable implementation.

School Discipline Policies

Discipline policies often are more political in nature than they are educational or therapeutic (Noguera, 1995). When a school, for example, takes a public stance of zero tolerance for a set of specific undesired behaviors, adopting policies and procedures that undermine or contradict such "get tough" policies is often political suicide. Once again, as we look at school-wide implementation, we must realize that no system will please everyone, regardless of its merits. The reality is that the use of physical security procedures and reactive exclusionary policies are associated with schools that are less safe and have an increased risk of problem behavior (Mayer & Leone, 1999; Skiba & Peterson, 2000). This issue is best approached via a campaign of public education to expel the myths and allow logic to attract a consensus of persons within the school to take the lead in facilitating meaningful change.

Most schools do engage in some instructional procedures designed to reduce the risk of challenging or dangerous behavior. Conflict resolution, restitution, character education, and a variety of other programs typically are implemented with a targeted student group or across the school with emphasis on a specific targeted group. Often, schools are quite invested in these programs and have data to justify their continued use. In some cases, schools might see FBA as a threat to what they have in place, looking at it as an "either–or" proposition. It must be stressed to schools that school-wide implementation of FBA does not preclude the use of any proactive or instructionally based interventions. Rather, FBA is a process that assists targeted programs and is implemented when students continue to have problems *despite* their involvement in these targeted programs.

However, it should be made clear up front that the FBA process will prescribe specific individualized intervention programs or strategies for these students who have failed. Existing school strategies will be a part of intervention for these students only when the FBA indicates that such strategies are a functional match for the identified needs of the student.

INADEQUACIES OF TRADITIONAL PROFESSIONAL DEVELOPMENT MODELS

As described earlier, traditional models of professional development are insufficient to address the need for ongoing professional growth, particularly for those trying to provide education and support to those children who manifest the most difficult behavioral problems. Many of the limitations are related to the organizational and resource challenges faced by schools and other provider agencies.

Agencies without large numbers of staff to be trained simply cannot generate enough "critical mass" for a state or regional PBS training team to justify committing large blocks of training days for on-site and follow-up support. These agencies often fall through the cracks unless they can combine with other small agencies to create the necessary mass. Some agencies, by virtue of geographical location (particularly in rural areas) have poor access to professional development resources.

Scheduling issues, especially with schools, wreak havoc when setting up professional development initiatives. Often, professional development specialists cannot negotiate effectively with districts or schools for release time that will enable teachers and other educational staff (administrators, teaching assistants, special education staff) to participate in instructional activities. Furthermore, there are added costs to acquire substitute teachers.

The sequencing of professional development to fit individual and organizational needs can be tough to agree on, including when to schedule days where several staff will be attending on-site instructional activities and how long these on-site activities will last.

Conflicts inevitably occur, creating problems related to attendance. In addition, designing the contextual features of a professional development approach that will address the individual needs of staff members can be difficult to achieve. Finally, staff turnover issues can be problematic when longitudinal PBS training commitments are obtained. Some staff begin the training but never complete it, whereas newly hired staff frequently are introduced in the middle of a professional development project.

Emerging Training Formats and Strategies

New professional development strategies, emerging from information technology, offer the opportunity to address the unique organizational challenges schools and other agencies face directly. One method for disseminating PBS that might provide solutions to some of the problems described earlier is the introduction of online instructional resources. Web-based professional development approaches offer significant benefits above and beyond traditional professional development strategies. Online instruction can provide teachers with new ways of obtaining information using flexible, self-paced instructional opportunities. Online instructional methods are now available for professional development specialists to design systems allowing teachers to actively seek feedback, advice, and support. This type of approach can be valuable when it is difficult to set up an on-site visit and respond in a timely manner to a stressful situation a teacher or staff person might be encountering. Online instruction can reach a large audience and might be much more responsive to the needs of agencies by promoting access and dissemination of crucial resources regardless of geographic locales. Examples of online instructional materials currently available in the area of PBS include a pilot module, Understanding Problem Behavior, developed at the University of Kentucky (www.uky.edu/~rljone00/pbis/), and a full set of courses on PBS developed by the Online Academy (www.onlineacademy.org) at the University of Kansas.

Online and Web-based training. The University of Kansas Center for Research on Learning, in partnership with the Kansas University Affiliated Program, received funding from the Office of Special Education Programs in October 1997 to develop, over a 3-year period, a set of instructional modules formatted for delivery over the World Wide Web in an online, interactive instructional format. Designed to be a method of translating research into immediate practice for preservice teacher trainees, these modules are being developed to address three content areas: teaching reading to students with learning disabilities, using technology in the classroom, and implementing FBA and PBS. This project, called the Online Academy, is designed to rapidly deploy information regarding research-based strategies to facilitate best practice instructional methods; curricular adaptations; curriculum-based assessments; and school, family, and community partnerships. The foundations for the Online Academy modules are (a) identifying promising practices that have been validated through rigorous research methods, (b) creating modules that can be combined to form online courses, and (c) establishing a system of pedagogy that permits preservice and inservice training to proceed at an individualized pace.

The vision held by the Online Academy consists of two parts. First, the Online Academy provides teachers with a flexible format for obtaining information about research-validated interventions. Second, the Online Academy is designed to provide opportunities for teachers to routinely access online instruction when they are in need of solutions for everyday problems in their classroom. The Online Academy modules were developed using a set of research standards with input from a jury of researchers, experienced instructors, and 1st-year teachers. These jurors were selected to assure that high-quality, research-validated interventions and strategies were designed so that the content of the modules would be appealing and useful for teachers. The Appendix presents the content map for the modular configuration of the PBS and FBA portion of the Online Academy. Taken as a whole, these modules capture the scope and "state of the art" of present research validated practices in FBA and PBS.

In compiling the content of the modules, the PBS research team at the University of Kansas proceeded on the basis of the selection standards presented in Table 1.

Fortunately, much that has been published in the psychology and special education literature on FBA and BPS has been characterized by scientific rigor and conservative influences drawn with respect to the limitations of the database from each study. As in all areas of new knowledge, however, some published information is documented insufficiently or includes results from poorly executed research and therefore should not be advanced to practitioners absent from further replication and research. The standards presented in Table 1 allowed the Academy to construct modular content for teacher educators and staff development that met strict standards for the advancement of research findings into practice.

Each of the instructional modules identified in the content map for PBS presented in the Appendix is designed to convey information interactively through auditory, visual, and print-mediated formats that are roughly the equivalent of 1 hr (or unit) in a preservice teacher education course. Thus, modules can be combined in groups of three to compose a college or university-level online, three-unit course for teacher education, or they can be configured individually for ongoing staff development with continuing educational units as an option.

Each module is composed of lessons that contain lists of readings, resources, audiostreamed information with graphics, specific practice exercises, self- or instructor assessments of skills acquired, and sources for more information. An additional module not shown in the Appendix is available for college and university professors in teacher

TABLE 1
Proposed Selection Standards

The research must have been conducted in instructional environments involving learners with disabilities.
The research must have been documented as being effective for learners with disabilities who are at risk for school failure.
The research must have been subjected to a documented external review process.
The research must have been disseminated or applied in a format that is designed for implementation by practitioners.
The research must be in an area of methodology or curriculum that generally is perceived as having a high priority need to improve practice.
The instructional resources used in the research must be available to the Online Academy.

education or staff development coordinators and instructors. This "Instructors' module" is designed to prepare instructors to respond to users online and provide technical assistance to users entering the modules for the first time.

As can be seen from the Appendix, the total content of the PBS portion of the Online Academy is exhaustive of the present state-of-the-art in FBA. It is designed to acquaint the beginner, encountering these concepts and practices for the first time, with awareness-level information and the desire to move along and learn more. It advances with each successive module to more sophisticated levels of knowledge and practice, and it increases in scope from single behavioral problems to comprehensive lifestyle changes. It encompasses singular applications of FBA to individuals as well as extensions of FBA and PBS practices to become the basis for school-wide discipline applications. In short, the content of the PBS portion of the Online Academy is intended to be exhaustive of research to practice in FBA and PBS to the year 2001.

The instructional modules created by the Online Academy are available to disseminate conceptual information to teachers and other service providers as one component of a comprehensive staff development approach. The pedagogy of online instruction enables participants to acquire knowledge in an immediate manner, as opposed to more traditional inservice training such as attending site-based courses or consultant-based instruction. Online instruction has the capability of reaching large numbers of individuals, in geographically diverse areas of a state, providing a continual source of knowledge.

The Online Academy modules can be accessed by any computer with Internet capabilities and contain several options for use. For instance, the Online Academy modules include an option for audiostreamed material that requires a sound card and the G2 RealPlayer software program. However, access to the materials is available through print media as well. The Online Academy modules accommodate different learning styles while maintaining Bobby Compliance, for access by persons with sensory disabilities, and maintaining a strong value on achieving high standards for written content. Because of the diversity in settings that support students with problem behavior, the Online Academy modules have integrated examples of PBS strategies used in a variety of school and community settings and with students of all age ranges, types, and levels of disabilities. Efforts have been taken to increase generalization of PBS strategies to the variety of daily situations and settings that teachers and other support staff encounter.

Interactive CD-ROM training. Recognizing the need for standardized, accountable, and accessible training by practitioners in procedures for conducting FBAs, faculty and staff at the University of Kentucky developed an interactive tutorial on FBA. Supported by a grant from the Kentucky Department of Education, a beta version was completed in the spring of 1999. Copies were distributed to all school districts within the state. It became apparent that the need for such a training package extended to the national level; therefore, a commercial version was developed and recently was published (Liaupsin, Scott, & Nelson, 2000). This module includes an overview of the process, a systematic tutorial through the steps involved in conducting an FBA, and case studies that allow participants to perform these steps with actual students. Currently, work is proceeding on the development of a companion CD-ROM on developing behavior intervention plans based on FBA.

CD-ROM training modules are advantageous in several respects. First, the CD-ROM drive is now a common component on the average computer, making this format extremely accessible to most school settings while maintaining portability. Second, the technology and cost required to produce CD-ROMs have come down to a level where they can be produced on a midlevel desktop computer (e.g., Macintosh G4). Individual CDs can be burned for about $1, making it affordable to continue updating content and individualizing examples for specific school levels (i.e., elementary, middle, or high school). Third, video can be programmed directly onto a CD, allowing for learners to view and review specific examples at their convenience. Last, effective use of instructional technology within the training modules allows for very interactive and engaging training and application exercises.

CONCLUSIONS AND RECOMMENDATIONS

We believe that preservice training, ongoing technical assistance, and practical demonstrations of effect will be needed to assure successful implementation of the FBA process. These issues have immediate implications for teacher education and the manner in which we train schools to consider and use FBA. Assuming that teacher trainers will accept FBA, its underlying philosophy, and the systemic manner in which it is applied is far more than a simple training issue. Yet, evidence suggests that, even if accepted, the current "hit and run" model of training and inservice, which typically lacks necessary technical support to maintain practice, likely will be insufficient to change school-wide practice. Systems change will require a consensus of commitment by those for whom the system is composed. The course of negative and exclusionary policy (i.e., suspending or expelling students) is easily returned to because such practices provide immediate reinforcement to school personnel by eliminating an aversive stimulus (the "problem" student). If more proactive approaches are to be maintained, they must be implemented with sufficient fidelity to demonstrate consistent and pronounced positive effects.

The new amendments to IDEA (1997) reaffirm a commitment to educating students with disabilities in inclusive settings. Although inclusion in general education classrooms continues to be supported for a range of children and disability types, it continues to be problematic for students with challenging behavior. The emphasis on collaborative practices has opened the door for a team approach to intervention planning. Interactive teaming has been advocated to guide practices in school-wide discipline (Colvin, Kameenui, & Sugai, 1993; Nelson, 1996), individual behavioral consultation (Lewis & Sugai, 1996), and effective behavioral support (Sugai & Horner, in press). However, these teaming strategies rely on collective brainstorming and input, as opposed to an individual "expert" model—introducing another change in the traditional system. Consequently, team-based intervention planning demands systemwide implementation, shared expertise, and adequate training in both intervention and collaboration skills.

Because FBA and subsequent functional behavioral interventions are best implemented by teams and established as processes across the school, training must involve all school staff members who will interact with students or have substantial opportunities to observe students in natural settings. FBA should not be seen as the role of the special education teacher, counselor, school psychologist, or other specialist. Rather, FBA must be conceived of and practiced as a schoolwide process. Although a teacher might ask for assistance in completing an FBA, the procedure itself should be seen as a normal part of the prereferral intervention process followed by all teachers. Because typically this is not the manner in which chronic challenging behaviors are handled, training requires schoolwide acceptance and commitment. This entails thinking about FBA as a proactive rather than reactive strategy. That is, FBA should not be thought of as being used solely for dangerous behaviors, or as a precursor to change in placement or school exclusion.

When used in a systemic and proactive manner (i.e., within a system of PBS), FBA should be used as a means of early intervention for students identified at risk for behavioral difficulties. When used in this proactive manner across the school, FBA can increase the likelihood of success across all students and decrease the need for more costly and less effective reactive (exclusionary) procedures.

Still, the 1997 amendments to IDEA mandate FBA as a reaction to extreme or chronic behavior problems. We believe that, although necessary in these instances, advocating the use of FBA only under these reactive conditions exemplifies a most inefficient use of the proactive technology. In an effort to maintain safe learning environments for all students while ensuring a free and appropriate public education for students with disabilities, the appropriate time to conduct an FBA is *before* the student has been suspended or moved to an alternative setting. Thus, training in PBS and FBA must be systemwide so that school staff might be aware of the rationale and skills necessary to implement effective screening and assessment procedures to prevent undesired behaviors.

Providing adequate training will require more than exposure to a single course or inservice workshop. Acquisition-level training should include peer coaching and teacher assistance team models and must provide practitioners with examples from their natural environment on which to work. As with any training, the more realistic training settings, the more likely it is that skills will generalize beyond training. Interactive training technologies, including online instruction, Web sites, CD-ROM modules, and online consultation are promising vehicles to allow practitioners to gain both concept acquisition and skill practice via an interactive format.

In summary, recent law requiring the use of FBA within a system of PBS presents several challenges to teacher education at both the preservice and inservice levels. Thus, we believe that the key to effective implementation of FBA will depend on our ability to create a comprehensive and interactive training package; justify our methods with logic, research, and real examples; encourage systemic implementation via collaborative teams; and facilitate successful outcomes via ongoing technical support.

Of course, whether the FBA process is ever used proactively in a reliable and effective school-wide manner will depend on whether this technology can be proven successful across all students. Our best shot at demonstrating this success likely will be with the same population of students that currently present the biggest challenge. We must implement FBA procedures proactively with students who demonstrate risk for violent and dangerous behaviors. Effective demonstrations with this challenging population will have the largest impact on practitioner opinion. However, if FBA is to be effective with these students, it must be proactive. Using FBA only under the letter of the law as a reaction to chronic problem behavior with these students will be unlikely to demonstrate the success needed to maintain its use on a more proactive and school-wide level.

We are confident FBA can and will be validated as an effective preventative approach to dealing with problem behaviors across the school. Our challenge is to train personnel to both accept and implement the technology with sufficient fidelity to ensure success. Further, we must continue efforts to produce and validate the most effective means by which these procedures can be understood, accepted, and implemented at the school level.

ACKNOWLEDGMENTS

This article was supported in part by U.S. Department of Education Grant No. H326S980003. The opinions expressed herein do not necessarily reflect the position or policy of the Department, and no official endorsement by the Department should be inferred.

REFERENCES

Anderson, J. L., Albin, R. W., Mesaros, R. A., Dunlap, G., & Morelli-Robbins, M. (1993). Issues in providing training to achieve comprehensive behavioral support. In J. Reichle & D. P. Wacker (Eds.), *Communicative alternatives to challenging behavior* (pp. 363–406). Baltimore: Brookes.

Carr, E. G., & Durand, V. M. (1985). Reducing behavior problems through functional communication training. *Journal of Applied Behavior Analysis, 18,* 111–126.

Colvin, G., Kameenui, E., & Sugai, G. (1993). Reconceptualizing behavior management and school-discipline in general education. *Education and Treatment of Children, 16,* 361–381.

Day, H. M., Horner, R. H., & O'Neill, R. E. (1994). Multiple functions of problem behaviors: Assessment and intervention. *Journal of Applied Behavior Analysis, 27,* 279–289.

Durand, V. M., & Carr, E. (1991). Functional communication training to reduce challenging behavior: Maintenance and application in new settings. *Journal of Applied Behavior Analysis, 24,* 251–264.

Foster-Johnson, L., & Dunlap, G. (1993). Using functional assessment to develop effective, individualized interventions for challenging behaviors. *Teaching Exceptional Children, 25,* 44–50.

Garmston, R. J., & Wellman, B. M. (1999). *The adaptive school: A sourcebook for developing collaborative groups.* Norwood, MA: Christopher-Gordon.

Gersten, R., Vaughn, S., Deshler, D. D., & Schiller, E. (in press). What we know (and still don't know) about utilizing research findings to improve practice: Implications for special education. *Journal of Learning Disabilities.*

Horner, R. H., Diemer, S., & Brazeau, K. (1992). Educational support for students with severe problem behaviors in Oregon: A descriptive analysis from the 1987–1988 school year. *Journal of the Association for Persons with Severe Handicaps, 15,* 125–132.

Individuals With Disabilities Education Act of 1975, Pub. L. 105–17, 20 U.S.C. § 1400 *et seq.* (Amended 1997).

Jolivette, K., Barton-Arwood, S., & Scott, T. M. (in press). Functional behavioral assessment as a collaborative process among professionals. *Education and Treatment of Children.*

Kern, L., Childs, K. E., Dunlap, G., Clarke, S., & Falk, G. D. (1994). Using assessment-based curricular intervention to improve the classroom behavior of a student with emotional and behavioral challenges. *Journal of Applied Behavior Analysis, 27,* 7–19.

Koegel, L. K., Koegel, R. L., & Dunlap, G. (1996). *Positive behavioral support: Including people with difficult behavior in the community.* Baltimore: Brookes.

Lalli, J. S., Browder, D. M., Mace, F. C., & Brown, D. K. (1993). Teacher use of descriptive analysis data to implement interventions to decrease students' problem behaviors. *Journal of Applied Behavior Analysis, 26,* 227–238.

Lewis, T., & Sugai, G. (1996). Descriptive and experimental analyis of teacher and peer attention and the use of assessment-based intervention to improve the pro-social behavior of a student in a general education setting. *Journal of Behavioral Education, 6,* 7–24.

Lewis, T. J., Sugai, G., & Colvin, G. (1998). Reducing problem behavior through a school-wide system of effective behavioral support: Investigation of a school-wide social skills training program and contextual interventions. *School Psychology Review, 27,* 446–459.

Liaupsin, C. J., Scott, T. M., & Nelson, C. M. (2000). *Functional behavioral assessment: An interactive tutorial.* Longmont, CO: Sopris West.

Mayer, M. J., & Leone, P. E. (1999). A structural analysis of school violence and disruption: Implications for creating safer schools. *Education and Treatment of Children, 22,* 333–358.

Nelson, J. R. (1996). Designing schools to meet the needs of students who exhibit disruptive behavior. *Journal of Emotional and Behavioral Disorders, 4*(3), 147–161.

Nelson, J. R., Roberts, M., Mathur, S., & Rutherford, R. B. (1998). Has public policy exceeded our knowledge base? A review of the functional behavioral assessment literature. *Behavioral Disorders, 24,* 169–179.

Noguera, P. A. (1995). Preventing and producing violence: A critical analysis of resonses to school violence. *Harvard Educational Review, 65,* 189–212.

Ruef, M. B., Turnbull, A. P., Turnbull, H. R., & Poston, D. (1999). Perspectives of five stakeholder groups: Challenging behavior of individuals with mental retardation and/or autism. *Journal of Positive Behavior Interventions, 1,* 43–58.

Safran, S. P., & Safran, J. S. (1988). Perceptions of problem behaviors: A review an analysis of research. In R. B. Rutherford, C. M. Nelson, & S. R. Forness (Eds.), *Bases of severe behavioral disorders in children and youth* (pp. 132–138). Boston: College-Hill.

Scott, T. M., Meers, D. T., & Nelson, C. M. (in press). Toward a consensus of functional behavioral assessment for students with mild disabilities in public school contexts: A national survey. *Education and Treatment of Children.*

Scott, T. M., & Nelson, C. M. (1999a). Functional behavioral assessment: Implications for training and staff development. *Behavioral Disorders, 24,* 249–252.

Scott, T. M., & Nelson, C. M. (1999b). Using functional assessment to develop effective intervention plans: A practical classroom application. *Journal of Positive Behavioral Support, 1,* 242–251.

Scott, T. M., Nelson, C. M., & Meers, D. T. (1999). [A survey of emergency and probationary teachers' perceptions of the match between problems in the classroom and their teacher preparation program]. Unpublished raw data.

Skiba, R. J., & Peterson, R. L. (2000). School discipline at a crossroads: From zero tolerance to early response. *Exceptional Children, 66,* 335–347.

Sugai, G., & Horner, R. H. (1999). Discipline and behavioral support: Practices, pitfalls and promises. *Effective School Practices, 17,* 10–22.

Sugai, G., & Horner, R. H. (in press). Discipline and behavioral support: Preferred processes and practices. *Effective School Practices.*

Sugai, G., Horner, R. H., & Sprague, J. R. (1999). Functional-assessment-based behavior support planning: Research to practice to research. *Behavioral Disorders, 24,* 253–257.

Turnbull, A. P., & Ruef, M. (1996). Family perspectives on problem behavior. *Mental Retardation, 34,* 280–293.

APPENDIX: CONTENT MAP

Module 1: Foundations of PBS

1. Overview of PBS.
2. Basics of Behavior.
3. Introduction to PBS.
4. Preventing Problem Behavior.

Module 2: Functional Assessment

1. Value-Driven Assessment.
2. Methods and Outcomes.
3. Indirect Assessment Methods.
4. Direct Assessment Methods.
5. Applying Assessment Results.

Module 3: Development and Implementation of PBS Plans

1. Design of PBS Plans.
2. Implementing PBS.
3. Modifying and Assessing PBS Plans.

Module 4: Intervention Strategies (Part I)

1. Setting Events.
2. Antecedent Interventions.
3. Replacing Problem Behavior.
4. Consequence Interventions.

Module 5: Intervention Strategies (Part II)

1. Social Skills.
2. Crisis Prevention.
3. Physiological Influences.

Module 6: Redesigning Environmental Systems

1. Classroom Management Strategies.
2. Staff Development.
3. School-Wide Discipline.

Module 7: Creating Positive Lifestyles

1. Person-Centered Planning.
2. Self-Determination.
3. Quality of Life.

For Product Safety Concerns and Information please contact our EU representative GPSR@taylorandfrancis.com
Taylor & Francis Verlag GmbH, Kaufingerstraße 24, 80331 München, Germany

www.ingramcontent.com/pod-product-compliance
Ingram Content Group UK Ltd.
Pitfield, Milton Keynes, MK11 3LW, UK
UKHW021958180926
475701UK00003B/73
9780805897326